THE EVERYDAY ENGLISH
HANDBOOK

THE

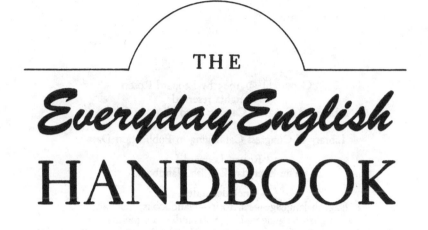

Everyday English

HANDBOOK

LEONARD J. ROSEN

DOUBLEDAY & COMPANY, INC.

GARDEN CITY, NEW YORK

Copyright © 1985 by Leonard Rosen
All rights reserved
Library of Congress Catalog Card Number 84-25938

Library of Congress Cataloging in Publication Data

Rosen, Leonard J.
The Everyday English Handbook.

Includes index.
1. English language—Rhetoric—Handbooks, manuals, etc.
2. English language—Usage—Handbooks, manual, etc.
3. English language—Grammar—1950—Handbooks, manuals, etc. I. Title.
PE1460.R58 1985   808'.042

Printed in the United States of America

Book design: Fran Gazze Nimeck

Quality Printing and Binding by:
Berryville Graphics
P.O. Box 272
Berryville, VA 22611 U.S.A.

FOR ESTHER AND SIDNEY ROSEN

Acknowledgments

This reference guide to grammar and usage has benefited greatly from the efforts of many professionals at Nelson Doubleday Books. I take particular pleasure in acknowledging the editorial expertise of Mary Sherwin, who with unsurpassing dedication labored over the many versions of the manuscript. Her requests for clarifications, restructurings, and rewordings were nearly always warranted and confirmed, once again, the importance of a writer's having a talented, interested reader to critique his work. Thanks to designer Fran Gazze Nimeck for her skill in bringing the chaos of the manuscript to a readable, attractive form; and to Marlene Connor for suggesting that I undertake this project. To Edward Zlotkowski of Bentley College, I owe a debt of gratitude for his advice on preparation of the final manuscript. And to Linda Rosen, my special thanks for the qualities that have made communication and my hours devoted to its study so very gratifying.

Contents

3. Phrases   38

4. Clauses   50

5. Sentences   57

PART TWO · USAGE

6. Pronouns   79

7.   Modifiers: Adjectives and Adverbs   89

8. Verbs: Tense, Voice, and Mood   96

9. Agreement Between Subject and Verb, Pronoun and Antecedent   110

PART THREE · PUNCTUATION/MECHANICS

10. Punctuation   121

11. The Mechanics of Writing   146

PART FOUR · EFFECTIVE WRITING

12. Eliminating Grammatical Errors   163

13. Improving the Clarity of Your Writing   180

14. Improving the Style of Your Writing   186

PART FIVE · PARAGRAPHS AND GROUPS
OF PARAGRAPHS

15. Organizing a Paragraph   201

16. Arranging Groups of Paragraphs: Writing Business Letters, Memoranda, Reports, and Compositions for School 226

A Note to the Reader

In the course of everyday conversation, you successfully—and repeatedly—employ basic grammatical rules. As evidence of your ability, try an experiment: Rearrange the following words until you have produced a coherent sentence:

million New approximately city seven in live York people

There are 362,880 combinations of these nine words. Let's examine two possibilities:

Seven York people live city in New approximately million.
City live in New York seven million approximately people.

These groupings don't make a great deal of sense; yet there are word pairs that sound familiar: "people live," "live in," "New York." As you can see, you do not unscramble a series of words randomly. You bring your knowledge of basic English grammar to bear on the task, understanding intuitively that certain words belong together and are placed before or after one another. Probably after just a few tries, you will arrive at a correct grammatical construction:

Approximately seven million people live in New York City.

Can you explain why you placed *seven* before *million* or why *live* follows *people?* If you cannot and your answer is "I just know —it sounds right," then you're in good company, for most people who speak English would respond the same way. The fact that you can recognize the proper grammatical sequence of words with relative ease demonstrates how much you already know about the rules of English grammar, even though you may be unable to recite textbook definitions of gerunds and infinitives. You have an *implicit* knowledge of your language.

This book will help you transform this *implicit* knowledge into *explicit* knowledge, so that you will be able to express yourself with confidence in situations in which a mastery of formal English is expected (e.g., business correspondence, business meetings, letters of inquiry or complaint, etc.). Confidence comes from being aware of the possibilities of language, from being able to speak about your writing in such a way that you can recognize problems and, through careful analysis, suggest solutions. In learning the vocabulary of grammar, you give yourself the tools necessary for improving your skills.

PART ONE

Grammar

1

The Parts of Speech: A Brief Review

As an architect, you wouldn't talk about a building you've designed without mentioning its parts. You might discuss building materials—bricks, glass, steel, and so on; or you might mention the functions of these materials—bricks form a wall; steel strengthens the roof. In much the same way, writers discuss sentences in terms of their parts and in terms of the functions of these parts. You might call a word a *noun* (a part of speech) or an *object* (describing the noun's function in a sentence).

Both the writer and the architect find it convenient to use a specialized vocabulary in discussing their subject matter. Architects speak of joists and bearing walls; writers speak of verbs and modifiers—the language of grammar. If you are a fluent speaker of English, then you know more about this vocabulary than you may realize, for you use the parts of speech *successfully* hundreds of times a day, even though you may not be able to recite textbook definitions of nouns and other parts of speech. Actually, there is no reason to learn the vocabulary of grammar unless you wish to *improve* upon your present skills, for then you will need to examine the components of sentences, how they operate, and how they can be reworked. This kind of examination requires that you be able to discuss your writing. A knowledge of the parts of speech and their functions allows you to do so.

NOUNS

The great *Pullman* was whirling onward with such *dignity* of *motion* that a *glance* from the *window* seemed simply to prove that the *plains* of *Texas* were pouring eastward.

STEPHEN CRANE

Each of the italicized words above is a noun—a word that names a person, place, animal, idea, or thing. Most sentences contain more than one noun; some sentences contain only a single noun.

The young *girl* went to the *store* with her *mother*.
The young *girl* slept soundly.

Common/Proper Nouns

Common nouns refer to a general class of persons, places, or things and are not capitalized. *Proper nouns* refer to a particular member of a class and are capitalized.

COMMON	PROPER
book	the Bible
railroad	the B&O Railroad
car	the Ford Mustang
woman	Marilyn Monroe

Concrete/Abstract/Collective Nouns

Concrete nouns name definite, physical objects. *Abstract nouns* name ideas, emotions, and qualities. *Collective nouns* name groups of people or things.

CONCRETE	ABSTRACT	COLLECTIVE
stone	truth	family
bridge	love	herd
chair	trust	team

Count/Mass Nouns

Nouns are classified according to whether or not they can be counted.

COUNT	MASS
one stick	silver
four hens	meat
seven violins	food

Nouns are either singular or plural in number. Plural nouns usually end in *s* or *es* (note*s*, book*s*, tomato*es*), although there are exceptions (child: children; alumnus: alumni; mouse: mice). Singular nouns have no special ending (note, book, tomato). Some nouns retain the same form in both the singular and the plural: one sheep, five sheep; one fish, ten fish. To be certain of the spelling of a noun's plural form, consult a dictionary.

Nouns can show possession:

William's coat   the groups' leaders

PRONOUNS

One of the most pervasive myths about sleep is that *everyone* needs eight hours of *it* per night.

In the above example, *everyone* and *it* are pronouns, words that take the place of nouns or pronouns in a sentence. *Everyone* is used here instead of a series of proper nouns (e.g., Jake, Linda, Mary, etc.) or a common noun (e.g., *people*). The pronoun *it* refers to the noun *sleep* and is used to avoid repetition of that word in the second part of the sentence.

There are eight types of pronouns, shown below with examples of each type. For a more complete list of these pronouns, see Chapter 6.

Personal pronouns (I, me, mine, my)

My shoulder aches during thunderstorms.

Reflexive pronouns (herself, himself)

Mr. Klein referred to *himself* as an honorable man.

Intensive pronouns (herself, himself)

The President *himself* attended the meeting.

Relative pronouns (who, which)

Alice Moore is the candidate *who* promises to reduce taxes.

Interrogative pronouns (who, which, what)

Who was knocking at your door at two in the morning?

Demonstrative pronouns (these, those)

These shoes do not fit well.

Indefinite pronouns (it, they)

They say *it* never rains in the Sahara.

Reciprocal pronouns (one another, each other)

Before parting, the players invited *one another* to their homes.

Like nouns, pronouns can be singular *(he, she, it)* or plural *(they, them)*:

She tells good jokes.
They tell good jokes.

Pronouns can indicate possession:

His singing voice is excellent.
Their children frequently misbehave.

Unlike nouns, pronouns change their entire form, not just their endings, to indicate their number (singular, plural) and function (subject, object) in a sentence:

Bob hiked through the Alps.
He hiked through the Alps.

Bob and Ellen hiked through the Alps.
They hiked through the Alps.

The Austrian mountaineering club provided Bob and Ellen with the appropriate maps.

The Austrian mountaineering club provided *them* with the appropriate maps.

For a full discussion of pronouns, see Chapter 6, pages 79–88.

VERBS

A verb is a word that expresses an action, an occurrence, or a state of being.

The wife of John Adams, Abigail Smith Adams, *protested* against the formation of a new government in which women would not be fully recognized.

In the sentence above, the verb *protested* expresses the action that a person has taken. In the sentence "The rock fell on his foot," the verb *fell* expresses an occurrence. State-of-being verbs —such as *appeared, seemed, was*—express the existence of a person or an object:

Mr. Humbert *was* happy.   Mr. Humbert *appeared* happy.

Tense

An essential function of verbs is that they indicate tense, revealing *when* an action occurs or when the subject exists in a certain state of being. (For a discussion of tenses, see pages 97–104.) The tense of a verb is indicated by its ending or the auxiliary that precedes it:

The present tense verb ends in an *s* or takes no ending:

When one has become an individual, one *stands* alone and *faces* the world in all its perilous and overpowering aspects.

ERICH FROMM

The past tense verb is marked by an *ed:*

Prehistoric artists in Tanzania, East Africa, *produced* records of various events in their lives by painting the walls of cliffs.

The future tense verb is marked by the word *shall* or *will:*

> The full importance of the computer revolution *will be understood,* perhaps, in fifty years—but more likely in one hundred.

Regular/Irregular Verbs

Verbs are either "regular" or "irregular" in the way they change form to indicate the past tense and the past participle (see Chapter 8). Regular verbs follow a set pattern, or conjugation:

I remember.	She believes.
I remember*ed.*	She believ*ed.*
I have remember*ed.*	She has believ*ed.*

By contrast, irregular verbs do not follow a set conjugation:

I eat.	She goes.
I ate.	She went.
I have eaten.	She has gone.

To determine whether a verb is regular or irregular, consult a dictionary, which will list the verb's various forms. (See also Chapter 8, pages 97–99, for a discussion of regular and irregular verbs.)

Auxiliaries

Auxiliaries are words that help to form certain tenses and moods. (See pages 108–9.) The future tense, for instance, takes the auxiliary *will* or *shall.* Verbs expressed in the subjunctive mood may be introduced with the auxiliary *would.* Following is a brief list of auxiliaries:

> do, does, did
> have, has, had
> am, is, was, were, been
> shall, will, can, could, should, would
> may, might, must

A single auxiliary can be paired with a verb:

By using satellite photography, scientists *have* created accurate maps of the ocean floor.

Often, two or three auxiliaries are joined with a verb:

Historians remark that John Kennedy *might have been* defeated in his presidential bid had there been no televised debate with Richard Nixon.

ADJECTIVES

I was wearing my *powder-blue* suit, with *dark blue* shirt, tie and *display* handkerchief, *black* brogues, *black wool* socks with *dark blue* clocks on them. I was *neat, clean, shaved* and *sober*, and I didn't care who knew it. I was everything the *well-dressed* private detective ought to be. I was calling on *four million* dollars.

RAYMOND CHANDLER

Adjectives describe nouns, answering such questions as *how many* and *what kind*. In the above sentence describing Chandler's detective, Philip Marlowe, what color is the suit? *Powder-blue*. What kind of handkerchief is Marlowe wearing? A *display* handkerchief.

Usually, nouns can be transformed into adjectives when their endings are changed:

fish   fishy
defense   defensive
beauty   beautiful

Verbs can also be changed into adjectives:

play   playful
enjoy   enjoyable
believe   believable

Occasionally, nouns are used as adjectives:

mountain lion   *grain* elevator

There are three classes of adjectives:

Limiting adjectives limit the meaning of a noun by showing either

> possession: *his* coat
> demonstration: *this* or *that* coat
> number: *one* coat

Descriptive adjectives comment on some aspect of a noun:

> *tiny* room
> *fabulous* painting

Proper adjectives are formed from proper nouns, and are capitalized:

> *Sunday* service
> *English* sheep dog
> *Russian* vodka

For a more detailed discussion of adjectives, see Chapter 7, pages 89–92.

ARTICLES AND DETERMINERS

> Scientists have discovered that *a* chimpanzee, using American sign language, can communicate *its* needs.

Articles and determiners are short words that help define nouns. As such, they are sometimes referred to as adjectives. In the example sentence, *a* is an article and *its* is a determiner.

There are three articles: *a, an, the.* The difference in meaning between "an experiment" and "the experiment" is substantial. In the first instance, one might be referring to any of a hundred experiments. That is why "an" or "a" is called an indefinite article. "The" is a definite article and would specify a single experiment.

The article "a" precedes nouns that begin with consonants or an "h" that is pronounced.

a chair   *a* history book

"An" is placed before nouns that begin with a vowel or an unpronounced "h."

an elephant   *an* hour

Determiners—*this, that, these, those, my, his,* and other possessive pronouns—are placed before nouns to indicate particular persons, places, or things.

her flowers   *your* flowers

ADVERBS

Marlon Brando *boldly* declared that Hollywood has no artists, only merchants.

Adverbs modify or qualify verbs. In the above sentence, the adverb *boldly* modifies the verb *declared.*

Your grammar teacher in the sixth grade may have said that all adverbs end in *ly.* Many do, especially the ones that describe an action, showing *how* the action gets completed. But many adverbs—such as *soon, now, sometimes, yesterday, tomorrow, there*—do not end in *ly.* Adverbs answer the following questions:

When has the action occurred?

Life insurance companies *presently* collect over one billion dollars per week in premiums.

How has the action occurred?

Marlon Brando *boldly* declared his views.

Where has the action occurred?

Mr. Keene pleaded for his life: "I looked *everywhere* for the jewels, but they're gone!"

How often does the action occur?

>   Cavities *frequently* occur between two teeth where food has been allowed to collect.

To what extent has the action occurred?

>   The office clerk *completely* misunderstood the recent directive.

Besides providing descriptive detail for verbs, adverbs also modify adjectives and other adverbs:

>   Nobody by sheer strength can "outfight" or "overcome" even a *moderately* heavy surf.   H. ARTHUR KLEIN

(The adverb "moderately" describes the adjective "heavy.")

>   Of all alcoholic beverages, wine is the only natural one—it will *quite* literally make itself out of grape juice.   WALTER S. TAYLOR

("Quite" can be regarded as an adverb since, in this example, it modifies the adverb "literally." "Quite" can also be regarded as a qualifier, a special class of words that modifies adjectives and adverbs, but not verbs.)

PREPOSITIONS

>   *In* the 1990s, when the sixth [computer] generation appears, the compactness and reasoning power *of* an intelligence built *out of* silicon [chips] will begin to match that *of* the human brain.
>   ROBERT JASTROW

A preposition is an uninflected word (it does not change its ending) that establishes a relationship between a noun and other words in a sentence.

>   built *out of* silicon   appears *in* the 1990s

The words *out of* and *in* are prepositions. Every preposition is followed by an **object** (in the examples, "silicon," "the 1990s")—a noun, or words functioning as a noun. A preposition, together with its object, is called a **prepositional phrase**. If a pronoun follows a preposition, it must be an objective-case pronoun: "for me," rather than "for I." (See pages 82–83.)

SINGLE-WORD PREPOSITIONS

about	as	despite	of	toward
above	at	during	off	under
across	before	for	on	underneath
after	behind	from	onto	until
against.	beneath	in	over	up
along	beside	into	through	upon
among	between	like	to	with
around	by	near	together	within

MULTIWORD PREPOSITIONS

according to	because of	contrary to	except for
in addition to	in spite of	on account of	with regard to

When the word "to" precedes a verb (e.g., to skate, to play), "to" is considered to be part of the infinitive form of the verb; it is not a preposition. (See pages 23–25 for a discussion of infinitives.)

CONJUNCTIONS

Conjunctions are words that connect and establish specific logical relationships between complete sentences or sentence elements. There are four types of conjunctions: *coordinate, correlative, subordinate,* and *adverbial.*

Coordinate Conjunctions

Coordinate conjunctions join sentences or parts of sentences that have the same grammatical status. Adjectives can be joined to adjectives, verbs to verbs, and so on. There are seven coordinate conjunctions:

and	for	or	yet
but	so	nor	

Each of these conjunctions establishes a specific relationship between the words it joins. For a discussion of these relationships, see Chapter 2, pages 28–29.

> George Washington used to take his false teeth out at night *and* put them in a bowl of Madeira wine.   GORE VIDAL
>
> The greeting card officially emerged around 1840 with the first published Christmas card, *but* it didn't become a mass-produced item until shortly after the Civil War.   CARL GOELLER

Correlative Conjunctions

Correlative conjunctions occur in pairs and, like coordinate conjunctions, allow a writer to join elements of equal grammatical status. The list of correlative conjunctions is brief. Notice that the meaning of each is unique:

either . . . or . . .   whether . . . or . . .
neither . . . nor . . .   not only . . . but (also) . . .
both . . . and . . .

Whether a cowboy has a lantern jaw *or* a chin like Slim Pickens, buck teeth *or* no teeth at all, a thick head of hair *or* nothing but imagination to run a comb through, his face will often have a weathered look by the time he turns forty.   JOHN R. ERICKSON

In the past several decades, wrestling has grown *both* in the number of participants *and* in the number of spectators.

Note that the presence of a two-part conjunction requires that words following each part be *parallel*—i.e., the words should be the same part of speech or should be phrased in the same way. (See pages 188–91 for a discussion of parallelism.)

Subordinate Conjunctions

Subordinate conjunctions allow a writer to join *complete sentences* by making one of the sentences grammatically less important than the other. As a result, one of the sentences becomes "dependent" upon the other, unable to stand alone as a complete thought. (See pages 50–54 for the discussion of dependent and independent clauses and pages 31–33 regarding subordinate conjunctions.) Following is a partial list of subordinate conjunctions:

after	how	since	until
although	if	so that	when
as	inasmuch as	that	whenever
as much as	in order that	then	where
because	provided	though	wherever
before	provided that	unless	while

If employees are given more generous benefits, they still may not use them.

Although Death Valley is famous for its brutal terrain and uninviting climate, campers can still exist comfortably there.

Adverbial Conjunctions

Adverbial conjunctions, or conjunctive adverbs as they are sometimes called, are used to join *complete sentences*. Sentences joined by adverbial conjunctions remain grammatically complete, able to stand alone, unlike sentences joined by subordinate conjunctions. (See pages 33–35 for a further discussion of adverbial conjunctions.) Following is a partial list of adverbial conjunctions:

accordingly	however	still
afterward	indeed	then
also	moreover	therefore
besides	nevertheless	thus
consequently	nonetheless	unfortunately
furthermore	otherwise	

A computer salesman receives some thirteen months of education; *afterward*, each salesman spends about three weeks a year learning updated computer applications and selling techniques.

KATHERINE DAVIS FISHMAN

For more than a century the slide rule was the essential tool of engineers, scientists, and anyone else whose work involved extensive calculations. *Then*, just a decade ago, the invention of the pocket calculator made the slide rule obsolete almost overnight.

ARTHUR C. CLARKE

INTERJECTIONS

An interjection is a brief, emphatic remark that is frequently followed by an exclamation point. When it is part of a sentence, the interjection is often set off by a comma:

"*Shucks!* I missed the lottery again."
"*Well*, you can always buy another hundred tickets next week."

THE PARTS OF SPEECH IN CONTEXT

While every word in the following paragraph has a grammatical name, we will examine just a few here:

FROM *Travels with Charley*

[1]When I was young and the urge to be someplace else was on me, I was assured by mature people that maturity would cure this itch. When years described me as mature, the remedy prescribed was middle age. [2]In middle age I was assured that greater age would calm my fever, and now that I am fifty-eight perhaps senility will do the job. Nothing has worked. [3]Four hoarse blasts of a ship's whistle still raise the hair on my neck and set my feet to tapping. [4]The sound of a jet, an engine warming up, even the clopping of shod hooves on pavement brings on the ancient shudder, the dry mouth and vacant eye, the hot palms and the churn of stomach high up under the rib cage. In other words, I don't improve; in further words, once a bum always a bum. I fear the disease is incurable. I set this matter down not to instruct others but to inform myself.   JOHN STEINBECK

ANALYSIS

1. The subordinate conjunction "when" combines two briefer sentences:

   I was very young and the urge to be someplace else was on me. I was assured by mature people that maturity would cure this itch.

   Notice that the pronoun "I" takes the place of the speaker's name.

2. The adjectives "middle" and "greater" describe the noun "age." Note the following auxiliaries: *was* in "was assured," *would* in "would calm," *will* in "will do."

3. "Still" is an adverb modifying the action verb "raise." Notice how the coordinate conjunction "and" combines two verbs:

   . . . still *raise* and . . . *set*

4. This sentence contains the prepositions *of, on,* and *under* and the articles *a, an,* and *the.* The sentence contains the following nouns: *sound, jet, engine, clopping, hooves, pavement, shudder, mouth, eye, palms, churn, stomach, cage.*

2

The Parts of Speech: Their Functions

When you use the labels "noun," "verb," and so on, you are describing or classifying individual words. But when you use a functional vocabulary—"subject" or "predicate," for instance— you are describing words of a sentence *in relation* to one another. Knowing both vocabularies will help you improve your writing, for you must be able to identify parts of speech in a sentence as well as their functions in order to analyze and then correct a problem.

Let's look at the difference between classifying a word according to its part of speech and according to its function.

> The snail won the race.
> The child dropped the snail into the sea.

In each sentence, the word "snail" is a noun, its part of speech. But "snail" functions differently in the two cases: in the first example, it's a *subject;* in the second example, it's an *object.* Following is a discussion of the various functional uses of the parts of speech.

SUBJECT

A subject is the noun (or any group of words taking the place of a noun) that produces or engages in the main action of a sentence. A subject may also be the person, place, or thing that the sentence describes.

1. Elsie smiled.
2. Milk cows that are properly fed can deliver up to eighty pounds of milk per day.

In example 1, the **simple subject** (the single noun about which the sentence is written) is "Elsie." In example 2, the simple subject is "cows"; the **complete subject** (which includes all the words associated with "cows") is "Milk cows that are properly fed."

PREDICATE

A predicate is a verb, plus all the words and phrases associated with it, that names the action engaged in by the subject or the state-of-being of the subject.

---

1. Elsie smiled.
2. Milk cows that are properly fed can deliver up to eight pounds of milk per day.

In example 1, the **simple predicate** (the single verb, including auxiliary verbs, that names the action or state-of-being of the subject) is "smiled." In example 2, the simple predicate is "can deliver"; the **complete predicate** (which includes all the words associated with "can deliver") is "can deliver up to eighty pounds of milk per day."

There are three types of predicate verbs:

1. A **transitive verb** transfers an action from the subject of the sentence to another person, place, or thing.

    Elsie *licked* farmer Jones.

2. An **intransitive verb** expresses an action limited to the subject of the sentence.

    Elsie *smiled.*

Many verbs can be transitive or intransitive, depending on the sentence in which they're situated:

You *should lock* the door.

("Should lock" is transitive, transferring action from "you" to "door.")

The runner's knee *locked.*

("Locked" is intransitive; its action is limited to the subject of the sentence, "knee.")

3. A **linking** or **state-of-being verb** (which is a type of intransitive verb) allows words in the predicate to describe or rename the subject of the sentence.

Elsie *appeared* contented.
The man on the left *is* farmer Jones.

Common linking verbs include the following:

is, was, were, have/has been;
look, smell, taste, sound, feel;
appear, seem, become, remain, stay.

Depending on the sentence, a word can function as a linking verb or as a transitive verb. Compare the following:

Alice *tasted* the ice cream.

("Tasted" is a transitive verb. The subject, Alice, engages in an action.)

The ice cream *tasted* delicious.

("Tasted" is a linking verb. The predicate adjective "delicious" describes the subject.)

DIRECT OBJECT

A direct object is a noun or a word functioning as a noun that receives the action of a transitive verb.

> The banker offered *the loan.*
> John ate *the apple.*
> The dog bit *the mailman.*

The direct object of a verb can be determined by rephrasing the sentence as a question formed with the subject of the sentence, the predicate, and the word *what* or *whom.* The answer to the question will be the direct object:

> The banker offered *what?* (the loan)
> John ate *what?* (the apple)
> The dog bit *whom?* (the mailman)

INDIRECT OBJECT

An indirect object may follow a transitive verb and be indirectly affected by its action. Most often, an indirect object follows the verb *buy, bring, do, give, offer, teach, tell, play,* or *write.*

> The banker offered *her* the loan.
> The cabbie did *me* a favor.
> The doctor gave *Mr. Scott* an injection.

An indirect object can be determined by rephrasing a sentence as a question ending with the words *to whom* or *for whom.* The answer will be the indirect object:

> The banker offered the loan *to whom?* (her)
> The cabbie did a favor *for whom?* (me)

Any pronoun that is used as a direct or indirect object must be an objective-case pronoun. (See pages 82–83.)

OBJECT COMPLEMENT

An object complement is a noun or adjective that renames or describes the direct object of a sentence. Most often, an object complement follows the verb *appoint, call, choose, consider, declare, elect, find, make, select,* or *show.*

> The judges appointed Andrea Smith *guardian.*
> The batter called the umpire *an unprintable name.*
> The concert made me *happy.*

In each example, the object complement completes the meaning of the direct object. (Notice that in the first sentence, the expletive "as" or "to be" could be positioned before the object complement, "guardian." See pages 71–72 for more on expletives.)

SUBJECT COMPLEMENT

A subject complement follows a linking verb and completes the meaning of the subject by renaming or describing it.

> The woman on the left is *Mrs. MacDonald.*
> The bishop appeared *pleased.*
> The patrons remained *calm.*
> Leslie is *twenty-one.*

The verbs in these sentences are linking verbs. They express no action; their function is to link the adjective or the noun in a predicate with a subject.

MODIFIERS

Modifiers are words that describe or qualify other words. They act either as adjectives (which describe nouns) or adverbs (which describe verbs, adjectives, and other adverbs). Modifiers can be single words, phrases, or clauses.

Here is an example of how sentences can be expanded with single-word modifiers.

Begin with a sentence that has no modifiers:

The boy walked.

Modify the subject with an adjective:

The *young* boy walked.

Modify the predicate with an adverb:

The young boy walked *quickly.*

Groups of words (phrases and clauses) can have the same function as single-word modifiers:

The *young* boy walked *quickly.*
The boy *wearing khaki shorts* walked *away from school.*

"Wearing khaki shorts" and the adjective "young" have the same function. They both modify the subject of the sentence, "boy." "Away from school" has the same function as the adverb "quickly": both modify the verb "walked."

VERBALS

Verbals are verb forms that function as subjects, objects, and modifiers. An *infinitive* is a verb form introduced by the word "to" or "in order to" (e.g., "to fly," "in order to live"). A *participle* is a verb form ending in *ing* ("breathing"), *ed* ("exhausted"), or *en* ("spoken").

Infinitives

• An infinitive can function as a **subject:**

To be or not to be is a question that has confused many people.

• An infinitive can function as an **object**:

Henrietta learned *to dance* at the age of three.

(The infinitive is the direct object of "learned.")

• An infinitive can function as a **modifier**:

That was a wine *to remember.*

(The infinitive functions as an adjective by modifying the subject complement "wine," which is a noun.)

The woods are beautiful *to behold.*

(The infinitive functions as an adverb by modifying the subject complement "beautiful," which is an adjective.)

The singer abruptly stopped his routine *in order to sneeze.*

(The infinitive functions as an adverb by modifying the verb "stopped.")

Because they are verb forms, infinitives have the following characteristics:

• Infinitives can express tense.

present tense	I would like *to go home.*
present progressive tense	I would like *to be going home.*
present perfect tense	I would like *to have gone home.*

• Infinitives can be transitive or intransitive. As such, they can be followed by objects or complements.

He hopes to buy *a hockey stick.*

(The transitive verb "buy" is followed by a direct object, "a hockey stick.")

She wants to be *happy.*

(The linking verb "be" is followed by an adjective complement, "happy.")

• Infinitives are followed by pronouns in the objective case:

Many people would like to be *him.*

• Infinitives can be modified by adverbs:

It is important to work *efficiently.*

(The infinitive "to work" is modified by the adverb "efficiently.")

He likes to sing *in the morning.*

(The prepositional phrase "in the morning" specifies *when* the singing occurs.)

• Infinitives can have subjects:

She advised *the prisoner* to refrain from any outbursts.

("The prisoner" is the subject of the infinitive phrase "to refrain from any outbursts.")

She wanted *him* to consider the gravity of his crime.

(An objective-case pronoun, *him,* is the subject of the infinitive phrase "to consider the gravity of his crime.")

Note: Infinitive phrases function in the same way as infinitives. See Chapter 3, pages 40–42.

Participles

Every verb has four principal parts—four forms from which the various tenses are constructed. These are the base or infinitive form, the past tense, present participle, and past participle.

BASE	PAST TENSE	PRESENT PARTICIPLE	PAST PARTICIPLE
stretch	stretched	(am) stretching	(have) stretched
speak	spoke	(am) speaking	(have) spoken
go	went	(am) going	(have) gone

Note that the auxiliary words "am" and "have" (forms of "to be" or "to have") can join with a participle to form the predicate verb of a sentence.

I *am stretching* to avoid muscle pulls.
I *have stretched* to avoid muscle pulls.

Now consider how the function of a participle ending in *ing* or *ed* changes when it is not used with an auxiliary.

• A participle can function as a **subject**:

Stretching is an important component of any exercise program.

• A participle can function as an **object**:

Because of a sore throat, Miss Jones was incapable of *singing*.

(The present participle "singing" is the object of the preposition "of." **Note**: Participles functioning as subjects and objects are called *gerunds*.)

• A participle can function as a **modifier**:

The *startled* intruder dropped the television and ran down the street.

(The participle "startled" functions as an adjective by modifying the noun "intruder.")

Because they are verb forms, participles have the following characteristics:

• Participles can take direct and indirect objects:

Ronald considered buying *his sweetheart a diamond ring.*

("His sweetheart" is the indirect object of the participle "buying." "A diamond ring" is the direct object of the participle.)

• Participles can be modified by adverbs:

Gently lifting the window, the detective slipped into the apartment.

("Gently" modifies the participle "lifting.")

• A participle can have a subject:

Albert's whistling could stand improvement.

(The gerund phrase "Albert's whistling" is the subject of the sentence. The gerund "whistling" also has a subject: "Albert's." The subject of a gerund is always expressed in the possessive case.)

Note: Participial phrases function in the same way as participles. See Chapter 3, pages 43–44.

Finite and Nonfinite Verbs

In the previous examples, both the participles used without auxiliaries and the infinitive form of verbs are called *nonfinite verbs* and function as subjects, objects, and modifiers. *Finite verbs,* which include participles with their auxiliaries, function as predicates in a sentence. Compare the following:

Jason *startled* the intruder.
The *startled* intruder ran down the street.

In the first sentence, "startled" is a finite verb and functions as the simple predicate. In the second sentence, "startled" is a nonfinite verb (a verbal) and functions as an adjective, modifying "intruder."

LINKING SENTENCE ELEMENTS

Coordinate Conjunctions

Coordinate conjunctions join elements that have the same grammatical status: subjects are joined to subjects, predicates to predicates, sentences to sentences, and so on. Coordinate conjunctions can join single words, phrases, or entire sentences.

Use the seven coordinate conjunctions to combine grammatical units in distinct ways:

And denotes simple addition:

John *and* Mary are friends.

But denotes a contrast:

Mary wishes to keep it that way, *but* John does not.

Or denotes a choice:

Depending on when you talk with him, John feels jubilant *or* miserable about the relationship.

Nor denotes a negative choice:

He does not want to lose Mary's company, *nor* does he want to continue moping around the house.

For denotes a cause (but not as specifically as the conjunction *because*):

His parents are pleased, *for* they had been concerned that his social skills were underdeveloped.

Yet denotes a contrast (and is more emphatic than the conjunction *but*):

They expressed pleasure at his affair of the heart *yet* remained discreet, for fear of embarrassing him.

So denotes a result or consequence of an action:

> After all, an adolescent has only one first love, *so* a parent is obliged to take it seriously.

Coordinate conjunctions are *misused* when they join grammatically equal elements that are logically incompatible:

> MISUSED: Lester went window shopping, but his car had not been returned from the garage.
> CORRECTED: Since his car had not yet been returned from the garage, Lester had time to go window shopping.

When two grammatically equal elements are joined by a coordinate conjunction, they are *compounded.*

COMPOUND SUBJECT:

> John *and* Mary helped themselves to a fifth slice of cheesecake.

("John and Mary" is a compound subject.)

COMPOUND PREDICATE:

> A well-executed Bavarian cream pie captures the imagination *and* delights the palate.

("Captures . . . and delights" is a compound predicate. Notice that each verb has a direct object, "imagination" and "palate.")

COMPOUND OBJECT:

> The chocolate mousse satisfied Linda *and* me.

(The coordinate conjunction "and" combines two direct objects: "Linda" and "me.")

COMPOUND MODIFIER:

> Jacob told a brief *but* poignant story.

(The coordinate conjunction "but" links two modifiers to the direct object, "story.")

COMPOUND SENTENCE:

Jacob told a poignant story, *yet* no one listened.

(This is a compound sentence containing two subjects, "Jacob" and "no one," and two predicates, "told" and "listened.")

Correlative Conjunctions

Correlative conjunctions join grammatically equal, parallel elements (single words, phrases, sentences). They occur in pairs and have a more emphatic impact on a sentence than coordinate conjunctions.

Both . . . and and **not only . . . but (also)** are more emphatic than "and"; they denote simple addition:

> *Not only* did Einstein develop the general theory of relativity, *but* he did so as a young man, in his early twenties.

Either . . . or is more emphatic than "or"; it denotes a choice:

> In any given season, a baseball fan can expect *either* the Orioles *or* the Yankees to play well in September.

Neither . . . nor is more emphatic than "nor"; it denotes a negative choice:

> *Neither* rain *nor* sleet *nor* snow can keep the mailman from his appointed rounds.

Whether . . . or denotes a conditional choice; it differs in meaning from "either . . . or" and "or."

> *Whether* the foreman hired the new mechanic *or* did not made little difference, since the shop was going out of business.

Subordinate Conjunctions

Subordinate conjunctions join independent clauses by making one clause grammatically dependent upon the other. The dependent clause is considered a grammatical unit and usually functions as a modifier.

Consider the following sentence:

The soldier returned home.

This group of words is a sentence, a complete thought. It is an independent clause that has a subject ("the soldier") and a predicate that completes its meaning ("returned home"). Consider what happens to the independent clause when the subordinate conjunction "after" is placed before it:

After the soldier returned home

The group of words is still a clause: it still has a subject ("the soldier") and a predicate ("returned home"); but the clause is no longer a sentence, since its meaning is incomplete. The presence of the subordinate conjunction "after" has made the clause *dependent* upon another clause for its meaning:

After the soldier returned home, neighbors came to visit and congratulate her.

This new sentence contains two clauses, one dependent ("After the soldier returned home") and one independent ("neighbors came to visit and congratulate her"). Notice how the dependent clause adds meaning to the sentence by modifying the predicate verb "came." *When* did the neighbors come to visit? *After the soldier returned home.* In this example, the dependent clause, considered as a single grammatical unit, functions as an adverb and modifies the verb "came." The dependent clause has the same function as the one-word modifier "yesterday" in a similar sentence:

Yesterday, the neighbors came to visit and congratulate her.

Consider another example:

> When man began to settle in villages about ten thousand years ago, he cleared the land in order to raise domesticated plants and animals.   STANLEY JAY SHAPIRO

The subordinate conjunction *when* has made it possible to join two independent clauses by making the first clause grammatically *dependent* upon the second.

> Man began to settle in villages about ten thousand years ago.
>
> He cleared the land in order to raise domesticated plants and animals.

The dependent clause *When man began to settle in villages about ten thousand years ago,* considered as a single grammatical unit, functions as an adverb and modifies the predicate verb "cleared" —establishing *when* man cleared the land.

Subordinate conjunctions can be classified according to the specific relationships they establish between dependent and independent clauses. Choose subordinators carefully.

To state relationships of *time,* use the subordinators *when, whenever, while, as, before, after, since, once, until.* (The dependent clause specifies the time that the action of the independent clause occurs.)

> *When Abraham Lincoln returned to the White House from delivering the "Gettysburg Address,"* he fell ill with smallpox.

To state relationships of *condition,* use the subordinators *if, even if, unless, provided that.* (The dependent clause provides the conditions under which the information in the independent clause should be considered.)

> *Even if employees are given more generous benefits,* they still may not use them.

To state relationships of *cause,* use the subordinators *because, since.* (The cause of an action or state-of-being in the independent clause is explained in the dependent clause.)

> *Because it is possible for presidential candidates to win the popular vote but lose an election,* political reformers have argued that the electoral process must change.

To state relationships of *contrast,* use the subordinators *though, although, even though, as if.* (Information in the independent clause is contrasted with information in the dependent clause.)

> *Although Death Valley is famous for its brutal terrain and uninviting climate,* campers can still exist comfortably there.

To state relationships of *purpose,* use the subordinators *so that, in order that, that.* (The purpose of an action completed in the independent clause is explained in the dependent clause.)

> The Panama Canal was built *so that ships could pass more quickly between the Atlantic and Pacific oceans.*

To state relationships of *place,* use the subordinators *where* and *wherever.* (The dependent clause provides descriptive detail for some element of the main clause.)

> The gypsy moth is native to Europe, Asia and Africa, *where its populations are normally limited by more than 100 natural predators and diseases.*   MARTHA TURE

Adverbial Conjunctions

Adverbial conjunctions, sometimes called conjunctive adverbs, join independent clauses and establish specific relationships between them. Both clauses remain independent and are joined with a semicolon or a period.

Adverbial conjunctions express five relationships between the clauses they join.

To state relationships of *contrast,* use the conjunctions *however, nevertheless, still.*

> During the summer in Antarctica (October to March), scientists flock to four observatories; *however,* when winter arrives, all but a hundred people head to more hospitable climates.

To state relationships of *cause and effect,* use the conjunctions *accordingly, consequently, therefore, thus.*

> Those who spend their winters in Antarctica must tolerate six months of perpetual night in cramped quarters; Navy psychologists *therefore* screen all applicants carefully before granting permission to stay the year around.

To state relationships of *condition,* use the conjunction *otherwise.*

> Anyone who lives with others in a confined, darkened environment must learn techniques for psychologically distancing himself; *otherwise,* he risks temporary madness.

To state relationships of *addition,* use the conjunctions *also, besides, furthermore, moreover.*

> The few who call Antarctica their home the year around speak of tense, sometimes violent experiences. They *also* speak of the deep tranquillity that is possible in so isolated a place.

To state relationships of *time,* use the conjunctions *afterward, then.*

> Enduring howling winds, invasions of privacy, darkness, and temperatures of minus one hundred degrees for months on end can profoundly affect an individual; *afterward,* many speak of their experience on Antarctica as the best of their lives.*

As shown in these examples, either a semicolon or a period can be placed between clauses joined by an adverbial conjunction.

*The above passages are based on an article appearing in *Science 84.*

Frequently, the conjunctions *also, therefore, thus, otherwise,* and *nevertheless* are not set off by commas when they are situated in the interior of a sentence. The decision of whether to have the reader pause at the conjunction (by using a pair of commas) is a matter of style. See pages 123–24 and 129 for the rules on punctuating adverbial conjunctions.

Unlike coordinate conjunctions (which must be placed between the words or groups of words they join) and subordinate conjunctions (which must be placed at the beginning of a clause), adverbial conjunctions may be shifted around in a sentence for effect. The placement of adverbial conjunctions in a sentence is a matter of style. Notice how the punctuation changes when the conjunction is moved to the interior of a sentence.

> Jonathan was one of fifty competitors in the triathlon; *however,* he was the only person over the age of sixty.

> Jonathan was one of fifty competitors in the triathlon; he was, *however,* the only person over the age of sixty.

> Jonathan was one of fifty competitors in the triathlon; he was the only person over the age of sixty, *however.*

SENTENCES IN CONTEXT

Every word in the following paragraph has a grammatical function; we will examine a few of these functions below:

FROM *Eleanor Roosevelt*

[1]The world that Eleanor [Roosevelt] came into appeared golden. [2]The average income for eleven out of twelve families in the United States was $380 a year, but people in the Roosevelts' circle built million-dollar homes and sailed on million-dollar yachts. It was a world full of servants, polo ponies, fashions from Paris and London, and the pursuit of style as a way of life. [3]Luxury was the background against which Eleanor's parents circulated as a young couple. They were part of the inner circle who were called "swells."   SHARON WHITNEY

From *Eleanor Roosevelt,* by Sharon Whitney. Copyright © 1982 by Sharon Whitney. Used by permission of Franklin Watts, Inc.

ANALYSIS

Sentence 1:

S	Mod	P	S Comp
The world	that Eleanor came into	appeared	golden.

The noun "world" and its article, "the," function as the subject of the sentence. Notice that because the predicate ("appeared") is a linking verb it is followed by a subject complement ("golden"), which refers back to and completes the meaning of the subject. The phrase "that Eleanor came into" modifies the noun "world.".

In the diagrams:
S = Subject   Mod   =   Modifier
P = Predicate   S Comp = Subject Complement

Sentence 2:

Notice how sentence 2 comprises two independent clauses joined by the coordinate conjunction "but." In the first clause, notice that two prepositional phrases ("for eleven out of twelve families," "in the United States") function as modifiers. The predicate of the first clause is the linking verb "was." It is followed by the subject complement "$380 a year," which renames the subject. The simple subject of the second clause is "people." It has two transitive verbs as predicates ("built," "sailed"), which are joined by the coordinate conjunction "and." The adjective "million-dollar" modifies each direct object ("homes," "yachts").

Sentence 3:

S	P	S Comp	Mod
Luxury	was	the background	against which Eleanor's parents circulated as a young couple.

The modifier, which describes the noun "background" and therefore functions as an adjective, is a dependent clause introduced by the relative pronoun "which." "Against" is a preposition shifted from the interior of the clause.

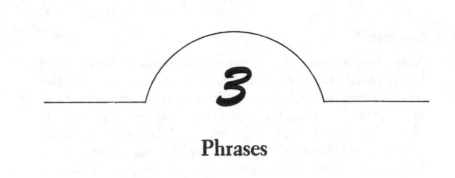

3

Phrases

A phrase is a group of related words that may contain a subject or a predicate, but not both. A phrase is considered to be a single grammatical unit and (with the exception of the verb phrase) functions in a sentence as a subject, as a modifier, or as the object of a verb or preposition.

Six types of phrases are considered in this chapter:

the prepositional phrase   the verb phrase
the infinitive phrase   the noun phrase
the participial phrase   the absolute phrase

PREPOSITIONAL PHRASES

A preposition followed by an object and its modifiers is called a *prepositional phrase*. Prepositional phrases function as modifiers.

* A prepositional phrase can function as an **adjective:**

At sixteen, Judy Garland was a well-known actress.

(The prepositional phrase "at sixteen" describes the subject of the sentence, Judy Garland.)

- A prepositional phrase can function as an **adverb:**

   A bicycle supports you *at three places:* saddle, handlebars, and pedals.

   ("At three places" modifies the verb "supports"—describing *where* the rider is supported—and functions as an adverb.)

   When lip-reading, a person is concerned *with the pronunciations of words.*

   (The prepositional phrase "with . . . words" functions as an adverb by describing the adjective "concerned." Notice that the prepositional phrase is composed of two shorter prepositional phrases: "with the pronunciations" and "of words." The second phrase modifies the object of the preceding phrase.)

It is common for prepositional phrases to be "stacked," with each phrase modifying the object of a preceding phrase.

   The dark caves where Tom Sawyer got lost, the courtroom where Tom saw Muff Potter tried, the drainpipe down which Tom slid for his clandestine rendezvous with Huckleberry Finn, all existed in the Hannibal [Missouri] of the 1840s and '50s long before they existed in Mark Twain's stories of the 1870s and '80s.

                                                           HAROLD HOLZER

Notice how the prepositional phrases are stacked, each succeeding phrase modifying the object of the preceding preposition:

   for his clandestine *rendezvous* with Huckleberry Finn

   in the *Hannibal* [*Missouri*] of the 1840s and '50s

   in Mark Twain's *stories* of the 1870s and '80s

NOTES ON USAGE OF PREPOSITIONAL PHRASES

- A pronoun functioning as the object of a preposition must be expressed in the objective case:

   Give the book to Frank.   Give the book to *him.*

- It is sometimes acceptable for a preposition to be situated at the end of a sentence when the sentence is reworked to form a question:

    I am looking *at this picture.*   *What* are you looking *at?*

A preposition should not be separated from its object by too many words; otherwise, the sentence becomes awkward:

    INCORRECT: *Which hotel* are we supposed to meet *at?*
    PREFERRED: *At which hotel* are we supposed to meet?

- A word that looks like a preposition, called a "particle," sometimes follows a verb and is considered as part of the verb:

check *out*	turned *on*	put *on*	looked *up*
check *in*	turned *in*	put *up with*	try *on*
handed *in*	handed *over*	cooked *up*	make *up*

To test whether *on, in,* etc., are prepositions or verb parts, take your sentence and rearrange its word order, placing the direct object between the verb and the particle/preposition in question:

    Marty *tried on* the suit.   Marty *tried* the suit *on.*

In most cases, if the rearrangement sounds natural, then the word after the verb is a particle and part of the verb. An awkward rearrangement indicates that the word after the verb is a preposition, as in this example:

    Mildred *decided on* the silk pants.
    Mildred *decided* the silk pants *on.*

INFINITIVE PHRASES

As shown in Chapter 2, an infinitive is the form of a verb introduced with the word "to" or the phrase "in order to" (e.g., "to sleep" or "in order to dream"). Verbs in their infinitive form are called nonfinite; they do not function as predicates in a sentence, but as subjects, objects, or modifiers. An infinitive with its modifiers, objects, or complements is called an *infinitive phrase.*

• An infinitive phrase can function as a **subject**:

> *To be awake* is to be alive. I have never yet met a man who is quite awake. How could I have looked him in the face?
>
> HENRY DAVID THOREAU

(The structure of the first sentence is a simple [if dramatic] way to make a statement. The infinitive phrase "To be awake" functions as the subject of the sentence; the second infinitive phrase, "to be alive," follows the linking verb "is" and serves as the subject complement.)

• An infinitive phrase can function as an **object**:

> Primitive man began *to form cultures during the Ice Age.*

(The infinitive phrase functions as the direct object of "began.")

• An infinitive phrase can function as an **adjective**:

> People these days have little time *to spend on activities that demand long hours and produce minimal results.*

(The infinitive "to spend" is modified by the prepositional phrase "on activities," which in turn is modified by the clause "that demand long hours and produce minimal results." The entire infinitive phrase, "to spend . . . results," describes the noun "time" and therefore functions as an adjective.)

• An infinitive phrase can function as an **adverb**:

> The modern American farmer not only votes for and organizes pressure groups *to promote his interests,* but also has an outstanding set of educational and scientific agencies that are publicly supported on his behalf.   CARL C. TAYLOR

(The infinitive phrase "to promote his interests" modifies the compound verb "votes . . . and organizes" by explaining the *purpose* of the two actions. The phrase therefore functions as an adverb. Notice that the infinitive "to promote" takes a direct object: the noun phrase "his interests.")

People who are ravenously hungry usually eat too fast *to notice whether their food is decently cooked.*

(The infinitive phrase functions as an adverb by modifying the adverb "fast.")

NOTES ON USAGE OF INFINITIVE PHRASES

- The infinitive marker "to" is sometimes deleted from a sentence to avoid awkwardness. The marker is most frequently dropped when an infinitive phrase, introduced by its subject (italicized in example), follows the verbs *bid, dare, do, feel, hear, let, make, need,* and *please.*

We heard *Mortimer* (to) sing in the shower.

("Mortimer" is the subject of the infinitive in this sentence. The infinitive phrase "Mortimer [to] sing in the shower" functions as the direct object of the verb "heard.")

SPLIT INFINITIVES

- When using infinitive phrases, avoid separating the infinitive marker "to" from the rest of the phrase:

    AWKWARD: We hope *to* in the next several months *see you again.*

    IMPROVED: We hope *to see you again* in several months.

- Infinitives interrupted by a single word may be acceptable; but whenever possible, avoid the split infinitive by transposing one or two words.

    MARGINALLY ACCEPTABLE:
    The director wanted *to* significantly *increase* the budget.

    IMPROVED:
    The director wanted *to increase* the budget significantly.

- Do not obscure or change the meaning of a sentence in order to avoid a split infinitive. The "marginally acceptable" sentence above is preferable to the sentence that follows:

    OBSCURED MEANING:
    The director wanted significantly *to increase* the budget.

PARTICIPIAL PHRASES

As discussed in Chapter 2, past and present participles form two of a verb's principal parts. Participles without their auxiliaries are called nonfinite verbs and function as subjects, objects, or modifiers in a sentence. A participle along with its modifiers, objects, or subjects is called a participial phrase.

• A participial phrase can function as a **noun,** in which case it is called a **gerund phrase:**

> *Overstretching muscles and tendons* can lead to tears and strains, which in turn can produce instability of the joints.

(The gerund phrase functions as the subject of the sentence. The direct object of the participle "overstretching" is "muscles and tendons.")

> Political considerations at the Olympics have kept athletes from *participating in sports.*

(The gerund phrase functions as the object of the preposition "from." "Participating" is modified by the prepositional phrase "in sports.")

> The ambassador resented *his not being invited to the state dinner.*

(The gerund phrase is the direct object of the verb "resented." Notice that the subject of the gerund is a pronoun in the possessive case.)

• A participial phrase can function as an **adjective:**

> The veil *worn by the bride* was a family heirloom.

(The participle "worn" is modified by the prepositional phrase "by the bride." The participial phrase "worn by the bride" functions as an adjective by describing *which* veil.)

Having called for early elections, the Prime Minister believed she could gain a show of support.

(Phrases that include past participles are often introduced by the auxiliary "having." Such a phrase placed at the beginning of a sentence functions as an adjective by modifying the subject, which immediately follows—in this case, "the Prime Minister.")

NOTES ON USAGE OF PARTICIPIAL PHRASES

• Like any adjective, a participial phrase is confusing when it is not placed next to the noun it modifies:

The trainer led the horse to its stable, *sweating profusely.*

Because of the misplacement of the participial phrase, the reader cannot be sure who is sweating profusely. Correct the error by placing the phrase (and all adjectives) next to the word it modifies:

Sweating profusely, the trainer led the horse to its stable.

• A participial phrase used as an adjective can cause confusion when the noun it modifies is not present in the sentence:

Resting in the shade of a fruit tree, the train pulled into the station.

Correct the dangling phrase by including in the sentence the modified noun (*Mr. Green,* in the example below):

Resting in the shade of a fruit tree, Mr. Green watched the train pull into the station.

VERB PHRASES

A finite verb (see page 27) is as easily extended into a *verb phrase* by adding auxiliaries, modifiers, objects, and object complements—or any phrases or clauses that can function as these. Observe how a single-word predicate can be expanded into a verb phrase:

Jack *returned.*   Jack *returned home.*

The verb phrase is extended again by adding a prepositional phrase that functions as an adverb, explaining *when* Jack returned home.

Jack *returned home after a hard day.*

A third modifier can be added:

Jack *returned home after a hard day at the pharmacy.*

An auxiliary verb can be added:

Jack *has returned home after a hard day at the pharmacy.*

The complete predicate of each of these example sentences includes the simple predicate, "returned," plus all the words associated with it.

In the following sentence, the verb phrase, or complete predicate, consists of the simple predicate, "revealed"; its object, "secret"; and the modifier of "secret," the prepositional phrase "of his birth."

The priest *revealed the secret of his birth.*

NOUN PHRASES

A noun with all its associated modifiers is called a *noun phrase.*

• A noun phrase can function as the **subject of an independent or a dependent clause:**

> *The photograph of a child wearing blue overalls* won first prize in the competition.

(The noun phrase consists of the simple subject of the sentence, "the photograph," along with a prepositional phrase, "of a child," and a participial phrase, "wearing blue overalls." Together these words form the subject of the verb "won" and of the independent clause.)

Alex did not attend the seminar because *a lingering cold* kept him in bed.

(The subject of the dependent clause, "because . . . bed," is a brief noun phrase. Notice that "lingering," which modifies the noun "cold," is a participle.)

- A noun phrase can function as the **indirect object of a verb:**

  The rescue squad offered (to) *each of the men involved in the accident* a woolen blanket and a cup of coffee.

(The indirect object is a noun phrase consisting of the pronoun "each," the prepositional phrase "of the men," the participle "involved," and the prepositional phrase "in the accident." The preposition "to" is implied, as is often the case with indirect objects.)

- A noun phrase can function as the **direct object of a verb:**

  The President addressed *the voters of New Hampshire.*

(The noun phrase is the direct object of the verb "addressed.")

- A noun phrase can function as the **object of a preposition:**

  At the height of *his career in politics,* Richard Nixon resigned from office.

(The noun phrase is the object of the preposition "of." The prepositional phrase "in politics" modifies "career" and functions as an adjective.)

See Chapter 5, pages 64–66, for a discussion of how noun phrases are used as appositives.

ABSOLUTE PHRASES

Absolute phrases are unlike other phrases in two respects: When functioning as adjectives or adverbs, prepositional, participial, and infinitive phrases modify individual sentence elements: subjects, predicates, or modifiers. By contrast, absolute phrases modify entire sentences. Second, prepositional, participial, and infinitive phrases contain a subject *or* a predicate. Absolute phrases contain a subject and a partial predicate (a past or present participle):

> *Her mission completed,* the botanist returned to the base camp.
>
> *The dust from the storm having settled,* William went to inspect the damage.

A sentence can be converted into an absolute phrase by deleting a form of the verb *to be.*

> Her mission ~~was~~ completed. The botanist returned to the base camp.
>
> ↓
>
> Her mission completed, the botanist returned to the base camp.

A second way to form an absolute phrase is to begin with a sentence that has a past tense or a past perfect tense verb as its predicate.

> His eyes finally *adjusted* to the light. William inspected the damage.
>
> The dust from the storm *had settled.* Frank left town.

Change the past tense verb or the auxiliary "had" of the verb in the past perfect tense to its *-ing* form, and place a comma between the resulting absolute phrase and the independent clause:

> *His eyes finally* ADJUSTING *to the light,* William inspected the damage.
>
> *The dust from the storm* HAVING *settled,* Frank left town.

(See page 124 for the rule on punctuating absolute phrases.)

PHRASES IN CONTEXT

Examine the phrases discussed in this chapter in the context of the following paragraph:

FROM *Sports in the Western World*

[1a.]Virtually every competitive sport in the modern world is a refinement [b.]of physical contests [c.]originating in ancient and medieval times. [2a.]Taking their form largely from primitive hunting and warring activities necessary for survival, competitive games began primarily as religious rituals [b]designed to win the favor of the gods or to honor the memories of heroic leaders. Over the centuries the sacred aspects diminished. [3]But whether in front of tribal totems, at the Egyptian temples to Osiris, beside Greek altars to Zeus, before the Roman pantheon, under the Mohammedan banner to Allah, or in medieval Christian monasteries and church cloisters, sports evolved always in relation to religious ceremonies, holidays, and institutions.

WILLIAM J. BAKER

From *Sports in the Western World*, by William J. Baker. Reprinted by permission of Rowman and Littlefield, copyright © 1982.

ANALYSIS

Sentence 1:

a. The noun phrase "Virtually . . . world" is the subject of the sentence; it includes a prepositional phrase, "in the modern world," specifying *which* "sport" (a noun).

b. The prepositional phrase "of physical contests" describes *what kind* of "refinement" (a noun) and functions as an adjective.

c. The participial phrase "originating . . . times" modifies the noun "contests" (the object in the preceding prepositional phrase) and functions as an adjective. Notice that the participle "originating" is followed by a prepositional phrase that functions as an adverb by describing *when* the contest originated.

Sentence 2:

a. The participial phrase "Taking . . . survival" functions as an adjective, modifying the subject of the sentence, "competitive games."

b. The participial phrase "designed . . . leaders" modifies the noun "rituals" and functions as an adjective. The participle "designed" is modified by two infinitive phrases ("to win . . . gods," "to honor . . . leaders") that function as adverbs, specifying *why* the rituals were designed. Notice that the infinitive phrases are joined by a coordinate conjunction, "or."

Sentence 3:

The main clause (underlined in the example) is introduced by six modifying phrases, each of which functions as an adjective modifying the subject, "sports."

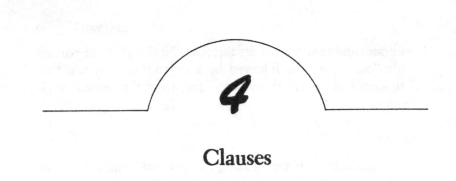

Clauses

A **clause** is a group of related words with a subject and a predicate that completes its meaning. An **independent clause** can stand alone as a sentence. A **dependent clause** cannot stand alone as a sentence, due to the presence of a subordinate conjunction (*when, while, since,* etc.) or a relative pronoun (*who, which, that,* etc.).

INDEPENDENT CLAUSES

Every sentence contains an independent clause, and every independent clause contains a simple subject and a simple predicate, which can be expanded with single words, phrases, and dependent clauses. In order to be certain that the group of words you are calling a sentence actually contains an independent clause, you must learn to make distinctions among sentence elements. One way to make these distinctions is to follow two basic steps.

Sample Sentence:

In 1930, Grant Wood finished his popular *American Gothic*, the painting of a dour, aged farmer who is standing with his daughter before a Victorian farmhouse.

1. Locate the clause(s) in the sentence by examining groups of related words and determining which have a subject and a predicate that completes its meaning.

   "In 1930" is a prepositional phrase.

   "Grant Wood finished his popular *American Gothic*" is a clause, which has a subject ("Grant Wood") and a predicate that completes its meaning ("finished his popular *American Gothic*").

   "The painting of a dour, aged farmer" is a phrase, not a complete thought. Though the phrase has a subject, it lacks a predicate that completes its meaning.

   "Who is standing with his daughter before a Victorian farmhouse" is a clause, which has a subject ("who") and a predicate ("is").

2. Identify the independent clause by determining whether it can stand alone as a sentence.

   "Grant Wood finished his popular *American Gothic*" is an independent clause. "Who is standing . . . farmhouse" is dependent, since it is introduced by the relative pronoun "who."

   Once you have identified an independent clause, you can be certain that the remaining words or word groups in the sentence will function as modifiers.

DEPENDENT CLAUSES

Two types of dependent clauses are considered in this section: those introduced by subordinate conjunctions and those introduced by relative pronouns. Both types function as modifiers, subjects, or objects in a sentence.

Clauses introduced by subordinators

after	before	unless
although	provided	when
because	since	while

When one of these or another subordinate conjunction is placed before an independent clause, the clause becomes grammatically *dependent* and must be joined to an independent clause. (See pages 14–15 and 31–33 for a more complete list of subordinate conjunctions and a detailed explanation of their use.) Consider an independent clause:

Erica went swimming.

By placing the subordinate conjunction "while" before the clause, the clause is rendered *dependent.* The clause can no longer function as a sentence; instead, it becomes a modifier and must be joined to a new independent clause:

While Erica went swimming, her brother lounged in the sun.

In this case, the dependent clause functions as an adverb by establishing *when* Erica's brother "lounged."

Clauses introduced by relative pronouns

who	whom	which	that
whoever	whomever	whose	

These seven relative pronouns take the place of subjects or objects in an independent clause. When the substitution occurs, the clause becomes grammatically *dependent* and must be joined to an independent clause to complete its meaning. (To select the appropriate relative pronoun for a clause, see pages 86–87.)

Observe how two sentences can be joined by using a relative pronoun:

The child is wearing overalls. The child is named Eloise.

By substituting the relative pronoun "who" for the subject of the first sentence, the sentences can be combined.

The child *who is wearing overalls* is named Eloise.

("Who is wearing overalls" is a dependent adjective clause— "who" is its subject, "is wearing overalls" is its predicate.)

Adverb Clauses

Although she was the junior member of the city council, Joan Simmons wielded a great deal of political influence.

(The independent clause "she was the junior member of the city council" is made *dependent* by the presence of the subordinate conjunction "although." The clause functions as an adverb by qualifying the verb "wielded" in the main, or independent, clause.)

The candidate changed his position *when public opinion polls indicated it was safe to do so.*

(The subordinate conjunction "when" makes the clause "public opinion polls . . . do so" *dependent.* The dependent clause functions as an adverb by modifying the verb "changed" in the main, or independent, clause.)

Adjective Clauses

You should indicate the place *where you want me to wait.*

(The dependent clause "where you want me to wait" functions as an adjective by modifying "place," a noun.)

The author De Silva wrote: "I have reached the age *when the longing to be great has been replaced by a desire to be competent."*

(The dependent clause functions as an adjective by modifying the noun "age.")

Annapolis, *which is the capital of Maryland,* is also the home of the U.S. Naval Academy.

(The relative clause functions as an adjective by modifying the noun "Annapolis." Notice that the relative pronoun "which," referring to the proper noun "Annapolis," serves as the subject of the relative clause.)

The President *whom I most admire* is Jefferson.

(The relative clause "whom I most admire" functions as an adjective by modifying the noun "President." Notice that the relative pronoun "whom" serves as the object of the relative clause. ["I most admire *Jefferson*" becomes *"whom* I most admire" once the pronoun substitution is made.])

Noun Clauses

Boy Scouts know *where they can find food in the wilderness.*

(The dependent clause "where . . . wilderness" functions as a noun and is the direct object of the verb "know.")

How Mozart composed symphonies as a child baffles me.

(The dependent clause "How Mozart . . . as a child" functions as a noun and is the subject of the sentence.)

Whoever answers the most questions in the least amount of time will be declared the winner.

(The relative clause "Whoever . . . time" functions as a noun and is the subject of the sentence.)

ELLIPTICAL CLAUSES

An ellipsis is an *omission.* In an elliptical clause, words have been omitted, though the meaning of the clause remains clear. The words most often omitted from elliptical clauses are relative pronouns and verbs in the second part of comparisons.

The President *(whom)* *I most admire* is Jefferson.
The story *(that)* *you told* frightened the children.
The Ozark Hardware stores are better equipped *than their competitors (are equipped).*

CLAUSES IN CONTEXT

Examine the clauses discussed in this chapter in the context of the following paragraph:

FROM *The Death of the Moth*

[1]Two summers ago I was camped alone in the Blue Ridge Mountains of Virginia. [2]I had hauled myself and gear up there to read, among other things, *The Day on Fire,* by James Ullman, a novel about Rimbaud that had made me want to be a writer when I was sixteen; I was hoping it would do it again. [3]So I read every day sitting under a tree by my tent, while warblers sang in the leaves overhead and bristle worms trailed their inches over the twiggy dirt at my feet; and I read every night by candlelight, while barred owls called in the forest and pale moths seeking mates massed round my head in the clearing, where my light made a ring.   ANNIE DILLARD

ANALYSIS

Sentence 1
INDEPENDENT CLAUSE: "Two summers ago I was camped alone in the Blue Ridge Mountains of Virginia."

SIMPLE SUBJECT: "I"

SIMPLE PREDICATE: "was camped"

Sentence 2
INDEPENDENT CLAUSE: "I had hauled myself and gear up there to read *The Day on Fire.*"

SIMPLE SUBJECT: "I"

SIMPLE PREDICATE: "had hauled"

DEPENDENT CLAUSE: "That had made me want to be a writer" is an adjective clause, introduced by a relative pronoun. The clause modifies the noun "novel."

DEPENDENT CLAUSE: "When I was sixteen" is an adverb clause introduced by a subordinate conjunction. The clause modifies the verb of the preceding dependent clause, "had made."

Sentence 3

INDEPENDENT CLAUSE: "So I read every day sitting under a tree by my tent and I read every night by candlelight." This is a compound sentence and has two independent clauses.

SIMPLE SUBJECTS: "I," "I"

SIMPLE PREDICATES: "read," "read"

DEPENDENT CLAUSE: "While warblers . . . feet" and "while barred owls . . . clearing" are adverb clauses, each introduced by a subordinate conjunction. The clauses modify the verb "read" in each of the independent clauses.

DEPENDENT CLAUSE: "Where my light made a ring" is an adjective clause modifying the noun "clearing" in the preceding dependent clause.

5

Sentences

The sentences that you write can be classified in two ways: by structure and by function. In terms of its structure, a sentence may be simple, compound, complex, or compound-complex. In terms of its function, a sentence may be a statement, question, command, or exclamation.

CLASSIFYING SENTENCES BY STRUCTURE

Simple Sentences

A simple sentence contains one independent clause.

The United States has an extensive national parks system.

SUBJECT:	The United States
PREDICATE:	has an extensive national parks system
SIMPLE PREDICATE:	has

Compound Sentences

A compound sentence is formed by joining two independent clauses, by either a coordinate or an adverbial conjunction.

One can hike through the arid lands of the Desert Game Range, in Nevada, or one can explore the sand dunes on the Pea Island National Wildlife Refuge, in North Carolina.

INDEPENDENT CLAUSE 1:	One can hike . . . Nevada.
INDEPENDENT CLAUSE 2:	one can explore . . . North Carolina.
COORDINATE CONJUNCTION:	or

Complex Sentences

A complex sentence is formed by joining an independent clause and one or more subordinate clauses.

When Congress passed the National Wilderness Act, it wanted to ensure that a rich variety of land types would be preserved by the the federal government.

INDEPENDENT CLAUSE:	it wanted to ensure . . . government
DEPENDENT CLAUSE:	When Congress passed the National Wilderness Act
SUBORDINATE CONJUNCTION:	When

Compound-complex Sentences

A compound-complex sentence is formed by joining a compound sentence with one or more subordinate clauses.

Because environmentalists and recent secretaries of the Interior have disagreed over the meaning of *preservation*, the government's control of the parklands has been controversial, and critics have charged that we are mismanaging our most precious national heritage.

INDEPENDENT CLAUSE 1:	the government's control of the parklands has been controversial
INDEPENDENT CLAUSE 2:	critics have charged that we are mismanaging our most precious national heritage
COORDINATE CONJUNCTION:	and
DEPENDENT CLAUSE:	Because environmentalists and recent secretaries of the Interior have disagreed over the meaning of *preservation*
SUBORDINATE CONJUNCTION:	because

CLASSIFYING SENTENCES BY FUNCTION

Declarative Sentences

A declarative sentence is a simple, compound, complex, or compound-complex sentence in which a predicate asserts or declares something about a subject.

Mrs. Henderson took her nephew, Eric, to the doctor's office.

(The predicate, "took her nephew . . . office," makes an assertion about the subject, "Mrs. Henderson.")

Interrogative Sentences

An interrogative sentence poses a question. There are two types of questions posed by interrogative sentences:

1. Questions that require a yes-or-no answer:

Was he happy?
Is she intelligent?

Note that the normal order of the subject and verb (a form of "to be") is inverted and that the subject is positioned between the auxiliary verb and the main verb.

Is he going?   Did he go?   Has he gone?
Must he go?   Would he go?   Can he go?

2. Questions that require answers other than yes or no:

When did Betsy Ross live?
How do Secret Service agents train for their jobs?
Why is blue cheese moldy?

These questions begin with the words *who, whom, which, where, when, why, how,* etc., followed by an inverted subject and verb (as shown above for questions requiring a yes/no answer).

Exclamatory Sentences

An exclamatory sentence expresses alarm, surprise, grief, anger, or some other emphatic sentiment.

"My goodness!"
"Ouch! Stop that!"

Imperative Sentences

An imperative sentence makes a request or gives an order.

"Nurse, call an ambulance."
"Calm down, son."

Usually, the subject of a command is not stated, in which case it is understood to be the pronoun "you." Sometimes, *nouns of direct address* ("Nurse" and "son," above) will be included in a command. The subject remains the implied pronoun "you."

THE FIVE BASIC SENTENCE PATTERNS

Sentences in English are constructed around five basic patterns, which can be varied in limitless ways. (See pages 62–71, showing how phrases and dependent clauses can be used to expand sentence elements.) Each pattern is an *independent clause* and differs distinctly from the others. The patterns are presented in terms of the parts of speech that constitute them and the functional relationships among these parts.*

*Use the following key to interpret abbreviations in this chapter:

N =	Noun	S Pred =	Simple Predicate
P =	Pronoun	D Obj =	Direct Object
V =	Verb	I Obj =	Indirect Object
Adj =	Adjective	Obj Comp =	Object Complement
Adv =	Adverb	S Comp =	Subject Complement
Art =	Article	Link V =	Linking Verb
S =	Subject	Prep Ph =	Prepositional Phrase
P =	Predicate	Infin Ph =	Infinitive Phrase
App =	Appositive	Part Ph =	Participial Phrase
Mod =	Modifier		

Sentence Pattern 1:

S	P
Elsie	smiled.

(INTRANSITIVE VERB)

N	V
Elsie	smiled.

Sentence Pattern 2:

S	S Pred	D Obj
The banker	offered	the loan.

(TRANSITIVE VERB)

Art	N	V	Art	N
The	banker	offered	the	loan.

Sentence Pattern 3:

S	S Pred	I Obj	D Obj
The banker	offered	her	the loan.

(TRANSITIVE VERB)

Art	N	V	Pro	Art	N
The	banker	offered	her	the	loan.

Sentence Pattern 4:

S	S Pred	D Obj	Obj Comp
We	appointed	John	secretary of the club.

(TRANSITIVE VERB)

Pro	V	N	N
We	appointed	John	secretary of the club.

Sentence Pattern 5:

S	S Pred	S Comp
She	felt	relieved.

(LINKING VERB)

Pro	V	Adj
She	felt	relieved.

VARIATIONS ON THE BASIC SENTENCE PATTERNS

By learning and applying four principles of modifying and replacing sentence elements, you can vary the five patterns presented above in limitless ways. You will want to vary these patterns if you find that the structures of your sentences are repetitive. Sentence variety helps to maintain the reader's interest.

Variation 1: Single-word nouns may be replaced by phrases or dependent clauses.

Nouns—which can function as the subject, object, object complement, or subject complement of a sentence—may be replaced by *noun phrases, infinitive phrases, gerund phrases,* or *dependent clauses.* These phrases and clauses have the same function (though not necessarily the same meaning) as single-word nouns.

EXPANDING NOUNS IN THE FIVE SENTENCE PATTERNS

Sentence Pattern 1:

S	V
Eddie	arrived.
The famous singer from Philadelphia	arrived.

(The noun phrase replaces the single-word noun "Eddie"; each functions as the subject of the sentence.)

Sentence Pattern 2:

S	V	D Obj
Boy Scouts	are taught	skills.
Boy Scouts	are taught	where they can find food in the wilderness.

(The dependent clause replaces the single-word noun "skills"; each functions as the object of the verb "are taught.")

Sentence Pattern 3:

S	V	I Obj	D Obj
The rescue squad	offered	them	a cup of coffee.
The rescue squad	offered	each of the men involved in the accident	a cup of coffee.

(The noun phrase replaces the single-word pronoun "them"; each functions as the indirect object of the verb "offered.")

Sentence Pattern 4:

S	V	D Obj	Obj Comp
We	appointed	Albert	president.
We	appointed	Albert	president of the club.

(The noun phrase replaces the single-word noun "president"; each functions as the object complement of "Albert.")

Sentence Pattern 5:

S	Link V	S Comp
Arthur	will be	King.
Whoever can pull the sword from this stone	will be	the rightful King of England.

(The dependent relative clause "Whoever . . . stone" replaces the single-word noun "Arthur"; each functions as the subject of the sentence. The noun phrase "the rightful King of England" replaces the single-word noun "King"; each functions as the subject complement.)

EXPANDING NOUNS IN PHRASES

Single-word nouns used as objects of prepositions, infinitives, and participles can be replaced by noun and gerund phrases and by dependent noun clauses. These phrases and clauses have the same function (though not necessarily the same meaning) as single-word nouns.

Prep Ph

Nelson is afraid   of snakes.

Nelson is afraid   of being bitten by snakes.

(The gerund phrase "being . . . snakes" replaces the noun "snakes" as the object of the preposition "of.")

Infin Ph

Hadley refuses   to eat meat.

Hadley refuses   to eat the flesh of warm-blooded animals.

(The noun phrase "the flesh . . . animals" replaces the noun "meat" as the object of the infinitive "to eat.")

Part Ph

Understanding talent   poses great challenges
                              to scientists.

Understanding the talent of child   poses great challenges
prodigies   to scientists.

(A noun phrase replaces "talent" as the object of the participle "understanding.")

Understanding   how child prodigies   poses great challenges
                 can write symphonies   to scientists.

(The dependent noun clause "how . . . symphonies" replaces "talent" as the object of the participle "understanding.")

Variation 2: Whatever its position in a sentence, a noun can be followed by an appositive. An appositive is a word or a phrase functioning as a noun that is placed after another noun or pronoun in order to rename or clarify it.

THE PLACEMENT OF APPOSITIVES

An appositive can be placed after a noun functioning as—

A subject:

N   App

Ted,   *a young dentist living in San Diego,*   is a close friend.

An object of a verb (including participles and infinitives):

N	App
I love Emilia,	*my childhood sweetheart.*

An indirect object:

N	App
The umpire gave Weaver, one last chance.	*the coach famous for his temper,*

An object complement:

N	App
We elected Koman to the presidency,	*the most powerful position in the union.*

A subject complement:

N	App
Farouk is a Republican,	*a firm believer in conservative politics.*

An object of a preposition:

N	App
Farouk is fond of Judith,	*his first cousin and oldest friend.*

THE STRUCTURE OF APPOSITIVES

• Appositives can be single nouns:

My daughter *Susan* just joined the Peace Corps.

(The appositive renames "daughter," the subject of the sentence.)

• Appositives can be phrases:

My job as a food inspector at the factory—*to open and inspect cans of tomato sauce*—quickly became a chore.

(The appositive is an infinitive phrase and follows the long noun phrase functioning as the subject of the sentence.)

• Appositives can be dependent clauses:

> The subject of the article, *how coffee harms the body's immunological system*, threatened to upset my morning ritual.

(The appositive clause renames the subject of the sentence.)

• An appositive can be emphasized by repeating (or by substituting a pronoun for) the word it renames:

> Florence Nightingale first described the basic principles of modern nursing in her book—*principles such as the importance of ventilation, warmth, and cleanliness in the sick room.*

(The appositive phrase renames "principles," the direct object of the verb "described.")

• An appositive can be further emphasized when it is preceded by one of the following words:

especially	including	namely	particularly
for example	for instance	such as	that is

> Allen likes chocolates—*especially ones with cherry cream filling.*

(The appositive renames "chocolates," the object of the preposition "of." Notice how the pronoun "ones" is substituted for "chocolates" at the beginning of the appositive.)

Note: See pages 88 and 122–23 for a discussion on punctuating essential and nonessential relative clauses, which applies to this discussion of appositives.

Variation 3: Nouns, verbs, adjectives, and adverbs may be modified by single words, phrases, or dependent clauses.

MODIFYING NOUNS
(OR PHRASES AND CLAUSES THAT TAKE THE PLACE OF NOUNS)

Single-word adjectives are used in the five basic sentence patterns to modify nouns. Phrases—*prepositional, infinitive,* and *participial phrases*—as well as dependent clauses can also function as adjectives and modify nouns. Following are examples demonstrating this point.

Sentence Pattern 1:

> Adj   S   V
> Amused,   Helen   smiled.

Replace a single-word adjective with a phrase:

> *Barely containing her laughter*, Helen smiled.

(The participial phrase replaces the adjective "Amused"; each modifies the subject, "Helen.")

Expand the phrase by modifying an element:

> Barely containing her laughter *over the actor's sneeze*, Helen smiled.

(A prepositional phrase modifying "laughter" is added to the participial phrase.)

Sentence Pattern 2:

> S   V   Adj   D Obj
> Raymond enjoys great   movies.

Replace a single-word adjective with a phrase:

> Raymond enjoys movies *of the silent era.*

(The prepositional phrase replaces the adjective "great"; each modifies the direct object "movies.")

Expand the phrase by modifying an element:

> Raymond enjoys movies of the silent era, *when facial expressions were an actor's principal means for conveying emotions.*

(A dependent clause, modifying the noun "era," is added.)

Sentence Pattern 3:

S	V	I Obj	D Obj
Industry	has given	Labor's recent proposal	serious
		(Adj)	attention.

Replace a single-word adjective with a phrase:

Industry has given Labor's proposal *to work a modified forty-hour week* serious attention.

(The infinitive phrase replaces the adjective "recent"; each modifies the indirect object "Labor's proposal.")

Expand the phrase by modifying an element:

Industry has given Labor's proposal to work a forty-hour week *in four days* serious attention.

(A prepositional phrase modifying the noun "week" is added.)

Sentence Pattern 4:

S	V	D Obj	Obj Comp
We	appointed	Miss Hanley	the industrial manager.
			(Adj)

Replace a single-word adjective with a dependent clause:

We appointed Miss Hanley as the manager *who would oversee the industrial accounts.*

(The dependent, relative clause replaces the adjective "industrial"; each modifies the object complement, "manager.")

Expand the phrase by modifying an element:

We appointed Miss Hanley as the manager who would oversee *both the domestic and the international* industrial accounts.

(A phrase modifying "industrial accounts"—the direct object of the verb "would oversee"—is added.)

Sentence Pattern 5:

S	Link V	S Comp
Max Lerner	is	the right person.
		(Adj)

Replace a single-word adjective with a phrase or clause:

Max Lerner is the person *to carry on the tradition.*

(The single-word adjective "right" is replaced by an infinitive phrase, "to carry on the tradition.")

Expand the phrase by modifying an element:

Max Lerner is the person to carry on the *liberal* tradition.

(The adjective "liberal" is added to modify "tradition.")

Observe how additional modifiers can be added to achieve even greater detail:

Max Lerner is the person to carry on the liberal tradition *of politics in Mason County.*

(The compound prepositional phrase functions as an adjective by modifying "tradition.")

MODIFYING VERBS, ADJECTIVES, AND ADVERBS

Adverbs modify verbs, adjectives, and other adverbs in the five basic sentence patterns. Phrases—*prepositional and infinitive phrases*—as well as *dependent clauses* can also function as adverbs.

Sentence Pattern 1:

S	V	Adv
Alfonso	argues	constantly.
Alfonso	argues	whenever the mood strikes him.

(The dependent clause replaces the single-word adverb "constantly"; each modifies the verb "argues.")

Sentence Pattern 2:

S	V	D Obj	Adv
Most bikes	support	you	comfortably.
Most bikes	support	you	at three places: saddle, handlebars, and pedals.

(The prepositional phrase "at three . . . pedals" replaces the single-word adverb "comfortably"; each modifies the verb "support.")

Sentence Pattern 3:

Adv	S	V	I Obj	D Obj
Yesterday,	Paul	found	his brother	a job.
After he had looked for six hours,	Paul	found	his brother	a job.

(The dependent clause "After . . . hours" replaces the single-word adverb "yesterday"; each modifies the verb "found.")

Sentence Pattern 4:

S	V	D Obj	Obj Comp	Adv
We	appointed	John	chairman	recently.
We	appointed	John	chairman	to enable him to preside at next week's meeting.

(The infinitive phrase "to enable . . . meeting" replaces the single-word adverb "recently"; each modifies the verb "appointed.")

Sentence Pattern 5:

S	Link V	S Comp
The mayor	was	hesitant.
The mayor	was	hesitant to recommend emergency procedures.

(The infinitive phrase "to recommend . . . procedures" modifies the adjective and subject complement "hesitant.")

Variation 4: Any sentence element or sentence can be compounded by means of coordinate, correlative, and adverbial conjunctions.

Subjects can be compounded:

Pat and Alan Smith went on a vacation.

Verbs can be compounded:

They *left* the kids behind *but called* frequently to check on them.

Objects can be compounded:

Sam told *both his mother and his father* to relax and enjoy themselves.

Complements and modifiers can be compounded:

"Everyone is *fine and happy,*" he said.

Entire sentences can be compounded:

"With the exception of a small fire, we haven't had a minute's trouble, *so* don't worry about a thing."

EXPLETIVES

Expletives are words that have no grammatical function other than to fill spaces created in a sentence when (1) the normal order of a subject and predicate is inverted or (2) an object complement is used.

"There" and "it" as expletives

"There" and "it" are the most commonly used expletives. When they appear in a sentence, the usual order of the subject and predicate is reversed.

S	V	Mod
A hidden staircase	is	in the wall.

Expl	V	S	Mod
There	is	a hidden staircase	in the wall.

	S	V	Mod
	To know where	would be	a good idea.
	the staircase is situated		

Expl	V	Mod	S
It	would be	a good idea	to know where the stair-
			case is situated.

The subject of a sentence containing an expletive remains the same as before the sentence's word order was changed.

Do not confuse the use of the pronoun "it" and the adverb "there" with the use of these words as expletives. In the following examples, "it" is a pronoun, the subject of the sentence, and refers to the noun "bottle." "There" is an adverb answering the question "the luckiest man in the world goes *where?*"

The pharmacist filled the bottle. *It* contained vitamin C.

There goes the luckiest man in the world.

"As" and "to be" as expletives

The words "as" and "to be" can be expletives in sentences that contain object complements.

The City Council elected Mr. Frank *as* interim mayor.
The City Council elected Mr. Frank *to be* interim mayor.

In the above sentences, "interim mayor" is the object complement. The sentence can also be written:

S	V	D Obj	Obj Comp
The City Council	elected	Mr. Frank	interim mayor.

SUMMARY

The goal of effective writing is not to write lengthy sentences, but to master sentence structures—matching length and complexity to the needs of the subject you're writing about and the requirements of your audience. (See Chapters 14 and 16.) Learning the five sentence patterns and the principles of modifying and replacing sentence elements will help you control the structure of your sentences, especially during the process of revising or editing. Typically, writers compose sentences that need to be reworked. Imagine that you had written the following:

The story is successful.

You are satisfied that the sentence is grammatical but dissatisfied with its vagueness. Familiar with the information in this chapter, you will realize that this example is described by Sentence Pattern 5:

Subject / Linking Verb / Subject Complement.

Consider the ways you can revise the sentence.

Expand the subject:

The story *written by Adrian Stewart* is successful.

Expand the subject complement:

The story written by Adrian Stewart is successful *because it recaptures the energy of youth.*

Compound a sentence element:

The story written by Adrian Stewart is successful because it recaptures the energy *and enthusiasm* of youth.

Substitute a phrase for the subject complement:

The story written by Adrian Stewart is *worthy of serious attention* because it recaptures the energy and enthusiasm of youth.

Compare the revised sentence with the original. Which is the more expressive?

The possibilities for revising sentences are limitless, once you appreciate the ways in which they are formed. As you continue to write and apply the principles of modifying and replacing sentence elements, you will undoubtedly discover your own distinctive writing style. If you are so inclined, analyze a sample of your prose to discover which of the five basic sentence patterns and techniques of substitution and expansion you use most often. If you are not pleased with your style of writing, work conscientiously to increase your repertoire of patterns and techniques.

SENTENCES IN CONTEXT

Examine the sentence types discussed in this chapter in the context of the following paragraphs:

Letter from Napoleon Bonaparte to Josephine,
April 3, 1796.

[1]I have received all your letters, but none has had such an impact on me as the last. [2]Do you have any idea, darling, what you are doing, writing to me in those terms? [3]Do you not think my situation cruel enough without intensifying my longing for you, overwhelming my soul? [4]What a style! [5]What emotions you evoke! [6]Written in fire, they burn my poor heart!

. . . You are the one thought of my life. [7]When I am concerned by the pressure of military affairs, when I am anxious as to the outcome of battle, when men disgust me, when I am ready to curse life, then I put my hand to my heart, for it beats against your portrait. . . .

By what magic have you captivated all my faculties, concentrated in yourself all my conscious existence? [8]It constitutes a kind of death, my sweet, since there is no survival for me except in you. [9]To live through Josephine—that is the story of my life. My every action is designed to the sole purpose of reunion with you. I am driving myself to death to reach you again. Madman that I am, I fail to perceive that I am constantly moving farther away from you.   TRANSLATION BY FRANCES MOSSIKER.

ANALYSIS

Sentence 1 is compound. The coordinate conjunction "but" joins two independent clauses.

Sentences 2 and 3 are questions formed by placing the subject, "you," between the auxiliary "do" and the verbs "have" and "think."

Sentences 4, 5, and 6 are exclamations. Sentence 4 is elliptical— the words "you have" are deleted, but understood. In sentence 6 the subject "they" is expanded by the participial phrase "written in fire."

Sentence 7 is compound-complex: The compound sentence is "Then I put my hand to my heart, for it beats against your portrait"—two independent clauses joined by the coordinate conjunction "for." The four subordinate clauses, introduced by the conjunction "when," function as adverbs and modify the predicate verb "put."

Sentence 8 is a complex sentence. Notice that a noun of direct address, "my sweet," separates the independent clause, "It constitutes . . . death," and the dependent clause, "since . . . in you." The word "there" is an expletive.

Sentence 9 has an infinitive phrase, "To live through Josephine," as its subject, which is repeated by the pronoun "that" in the second part of the sentence.

PART TWO

Usage

6

Pronouns

A pronoun's **case** describes its function in a sentence:

CASE	PRONOUNS	FUNCTION
subjective	I, we, you, he, she, it, they	subject of an independent or dependent clause
objective	me, us, you, him, her, it, them	object of a verb, preposition, or infinitive
possessive	my, mine, our, ours, your, yours, his, her, hers, its, their, theirs	expresses ownership

Within the three cases of pronouns, there are three distinctions one can make. Pronouns indicate *person, number,* and *gender:*

Person indicates whether the pronoun is referring to the person who is speaking, the one who is spoken to, or the one who is spoken about.

FIRST PERSON: *I* went to the store.
SECOND PERSON: *You* went to the store.
THIRD PERSON: *She* went to the store.

Number indicates whether the pronoun refers to a singular or a plural noun.

SINGULAR: *She* bought a sandwich.
PLURAL: *They* bought a sandwich.

79

Gender indicates whether the noun referred to is male, female, or gender-free.

MASCULINE: *He* is a professional wrestler.
                 Give *him* the apple.
                 His back ached from shoveling snow.

FEMININE: *She* is an accomplished architect.
                 Her brother arrived on Tuesday.
                 The book is *hers*.

GENDER-FREE: *It* was the rarest gemstone ever found.

There are eight types of pronouns in English:

PERSONAL: *I* hate sour cream.

REFLEXIVE: The fool shot *himself* in the foot.

DEMONSTRATIVE: *These* are my favorite chocolates.

INDEFINITE: *They* say that hard work never killed an honest man.

RELATIVE: The President *whom* I admire most is Jefferson.

INTENSIVE: The President *himself* attended the meeting.

INTERROGATIVE: *Who* was knocking at your door?

RECIPROCAL: The players invited *one another* to their homes.

Of these, personal pronouns change form depending upon their use in a sentence.

PERSONAL PRONOUNS

The Subjective Case

	SINGULAR	PLURAL
FIRST PERSON	I	we
SECOND PERSON	you	you
THIRD PERSON	he, she, it	they

• A subjective case pronoun can be used as the subject of a sentence. When using pronouns in a compound subject, be sure that the pronouns are expressed in the subjective case.

> *We* went to the concert.
> *You* should be more careful.
> *He* is a good friend.
> Freddy and *she* stopped by for a visit.

• A subjective case pronoun can be the subject complement of a sentence, following the linking verb *to be* (expressed in the forms *is, are, was,* and *were*).

> This is *she.*   It is *I.*

(The pronouns *she* and *I* take the place of proper nouns, such as Susan or Adrienne, which rename the subjects of the sentences, "this" and "it.")

• When a pronoun functions as a subject in the second part of a comparison, use the subjective case. (The words in parentheses are implied by the comparison.)

> Barbara can paint more efficiently than *he* (can paint).
> Steven is as fearless as *she* (is fearless).
> Benny remembered Eric better than *I* (remembered Eric).
>   BUT
> Benny remembered Eric better than (he remembered) *me.*

(Note the difference in meaning between the last two sentences. In the final sentence, an objective case pronoun, "me," is used, since it is the object of the unstated verb, "remembered.")

• When a pronoun is part of an appositive phrase that renames the subject of a sentence, use the subjective case:

> The committee—Jeanette, Linda, and *I*—took the afternoon off and went to lunch.

(The appositive renames the subject "committee." Therefore, a subjective case pronoun, "I," must be used in the appositive.)

The Objective Case

	SINGULAR	PLURAL
FIRST PERSON	me	us
SECOND PERSON	you	you
THIRD PERSON	him, her, it	them

- Use objective case pronouns as direct and indirect objects of verbs and as objects of infinitives and prepositions.

  The magician sawed *him* in half. ("him" is a direct object)

  The queen granted *her* an audience. ("her" is an indirect object)

  The ambassador tried to help *them*. ("them" is the object of an infinitive)

  The campaign committee had a surprise waiting for *us*. ("us" is the object of a preposition)

  Between *you and me*, we don't get enough vacation on this job. ("you and me" is the compound object of a preposition)

Note: When an infinitive phrase follows verbs such as *asked, advised, tried,* and *wanted,* the infinitive takes a subject. The subject of an infinitive phrase is expressed in the objective case, since the entire phrase functions as an object.

  The President wanted *him* to go on a clandestine mission.

  The counselor advised *them* to be patient.

- When a pronoun functions as the object of a verb in the second part of a comparison, use the objective case. (The words in parentheses are implied by the comparison.)

  The judge believed her more than (he believed) *me*.

  Benny remembered Eric better than (he remembered) *us*.

  BUT

  Benny remembered Eric better than *I* (remembered Eric).

(In this last sentence, "I" functions as a subject. In the preceding sentences, "me" and "us" function as objects of verbs.)

- When a pronoun is part of an appositive phrase that renames an object, use the objective case:

The commission hired a dozen consultants, including Francis Ringer and *me*.

The Vice-President took the committee—Jeanette, Linda, and *me*—to the meeting.

(In these sentences, the appositive phrases rename nouns, *consultants* and *committee*, that function as direct objects. Therefore, an objective case pronoun, *me*, must be used in the appositives.)

The Possessive Case

	SINGULAR	PLURAL
FIRST PERSON	my, mine	our, ours
SECOND PERSON	your, yours	your, yours
THIRD PERSON	his, her, hers, its	their, theirs

• Possessive pronouns are used to show ownership. When using a pronoun in a compound subject that shows possession, the personal pronoun is expressed in the possessive case.

This is *her* book.
Both *his* and William's privacy should be respected.

(When a possessive pronoun is placed before a noun, it may be called a *determiner* or an *adjective*.)

• No apostrophe is used for the possessive form of a pronoun.

The book is *hers*. The book is *theirs*.

• Possessive pronouns are used as the subjects of gerund phrases.

Their traveling to South America for the first time at the age of eighty demonstrated a hearty will to live.

(The gerund phrase "Their . . . eighty" functions as the subject of the sentence.)

No one dreamed of *his* sailing around the world single-handedly.

(The gerund phrase "his . . . single-handedly" functions as the object of the preposition "of.")

REFLEXIVE PRONOUNS

A reflexive pronoun renames the subject of a sentence. It is formed by joining the suffix *-self* (or *-selves*) to the personal pronoun *my, him, her, our, your, it,* or *them* and to the indefinite pronoun *one:*

herself	itself	oneself	themselves	yourselves
himself	myself	ourselves	yourself	

* The reflexive pronoun commonly functions as a direct or indirect object:

  The suspect surrendered *himself* to the police. (direct object)
  I gave *myself* quite a scare. (indirect object)

* Reflexive pronouns, placed directly after nouns, emphasize them and are called *intensive* pronouns:

  The teachers *themselves* couldn't understand the new ruling.
  The King *himself* made a plea to the people.

Note: Do not use reflexive pronouns in place of "I" or "me":

NOT	Aleta and *myself* walked to the market.
BUT	Aleta and *I* walked to the market.
NOT	Take *myself* as an example.
BUT	Take *me* as an example.

DEMONSTRATIVE PRONOUNS

A demonstrative pronoun is used in pointing to a noun. There are four demonstrative pronouns: *this, that, these, those.*

This belongs to you.
That is the bridge I was talking about.
These are the people who control the fate of our country.
Those are the fastest cars on the road.

INDEFINITE PRONOUNS

all	either	most
another	enough	none
any	everyone	no one
anything	everything	nothing
both	few	one
each	it	someone
each one	many	they

Indefinite pronouns, unlike personal, relative, reflexive, and demonstrative pronouns, have no specific reference. There is no one definite person, place, or thing in a sentence to which an indefinite pronoun refers. Avoid the indefinite uses of "it" and "they" in all but the most casual contexts.

One never knows when lightning will strike.
Someone will have to clean up this mess.
Everything was in perfect condition.

RELATIVE PRONOUNS

who	whoever	whose	that
whom	whomever	which	

Like any pronoun, relative pronouns can be substituted for nouns and other pronouns that function as subjects or objects in a sentence. When this substitution occurs, a group of words that had been an independent clause becomes dependent and will usually function as an adjective. The clause must be joined to a new sentence. Relative pronouns are especially useful for combining sentences in which one word or phrase is repeated.

Begin with two sentences you wish to combine:

The letter arrived Saturday.
The letter had been postmarked in Miami.

Substitute a relative pronoun for a word or phrase appearing in both sentences.

> *which* arrived Saturday
> The letter had been postmarked in Miami.

Embed the now-dependent clause into the second sentence, following the word it will modify.

> The letter, *which arrived Saturday*, had been postmarked in Miami.

Another example:

Begin with two sentences.

> Weather tends to be variable in Alpine climates.
> Weather becomes more extreme with increases in altitude.

Substitute a relative pronoun for a word or phrase repeated in both sentences.

> *which* tends to be variable in Alpine climates
> Weather becomes more extreme with increases in altitude.

Embed the now-dependent clause into the second sentence, following the word it will modify.

> Weather, *which tends to be variable in Alpine climates*, becomes more extreme with increases in altitude.

Rules of Usage

- Use the pronouns **who** and **whom** when referring to beings that possess a consciousness: people, a divinity, and animals (when personified).

> Peter Rabbit, *who* has been loved by generations of children, was born out of a series of letters written in 1893 by Beatrix Potter to the sick children of her former governess.   LOIS DECKER O'NEIL

• When using a relative pronoun to combine sentences, distinguish between the uses of *who* and *whom*.

Use **who** to replace a noun that functions as a subject:

Benjamin Franklin is considered one of the most important men of American science.

Benjamin Franklin is known to many as a great statesman.

Benjamin Franklin, *who* is known to many as a great statesman, is considered one of the most important men of American science.

(The pronoun *who* functions as the subject of the clause "who is known to many as a great statesman" and replaces the subject, "Benjamin Franklin.")

Use **whom** to replace a noun that functions as an object of a verb, infinitive, or preposition.

I admire Sandra Day O'Connor immensely.

Sandra Day O'Connor is our first female justice on the Supreme Court.

Sandra Day O'Connor, *whom* I admire immensely, is our first female justice on the Supreme Court.

(The pronoun *whom* replaces "Sandra Day O'Connor," a noun that functions as the direct object of the verb "admire." Notice in this example that the relative pronoun must be shifted to the beginning of the dependent clause in order to join the clause to a new sentence.)

• Use the pronoun **that** when referring to persons, animals, or things in an essential relative clause.

The stone *that* rolled onto his foot weighed two hundred pounds.

• Use the pronoun **which** when referring to animals and things in a nonessential relative clause.

Annapolis, *which* is the capital of Maryland, is also the home of the U.S. Naval Academy.

Essential and Nonessential Relative Clauses

Relative clauses usually function as modifiers describing nouns (that is, as adjectives). At times, these adjective clauses provide *essential* information for identifying a noun; at times, they provide *nonessential* information. (Essential relative clauses are sometimes called restrictive; nonessential relative clauses, nonrestrictive.) A writer indicates whether a relative clause is essential or nonessential by his use of commas.

Essential relative clauses—*never* separated from the rest of a sentence by commas—are used to define nouns whose meanings are unclear, given the context of a passage. In the example below, the relative clause identifies which children were rewarded.

The children *who helped clean up after the storm* were rewarded.

(Meaning: *Only* children who helped clean up were rewarded.)

Essential relative clauses typically follow common nouns—whose meanings are so general that they need further clarification.

Girls *who excel as high jumpers* are sometimes outstanding sprinters or hurdlers as well.   GEORGE SULLIVAN

The relative pronoun **that** always indicates an essential clause.

The age *that witnessed the opening up of the New World . . .* was a   time of great opportunity and rapid progress. RONALD JESSUP

Nonessential relative clauses are always separated from a sentence by a pair of commas. They are used when the context of a passage has already adequately defined a noun, so that the information in the relative clause provides interesting but not essential information. Nonessential relative clauses typically follow proper nouns or specific dates.

Her Uncle James, *who is ninety-one years old,* spends most of his time gardening.

Large crowds gather at Stonehenge for the sunrise on June 22, *which is the first day of summer.*

7

Modifiers: Adjectives and Adverbs

ADJECTIVES

Adjectives modify or describe nouns by answering such questions as "How many?" and "What kind?"

three mice	a *modest* proposal
a *tasty* meal	an *unconvincing* excuse
an *elaborate* hoax	an *enigmatic* smile

Many adjectives are "pure" in form; that is, they are not derived from other parts of speech:

tiny	sly	bad	little	simple	complex
happy	sad	weak	smart	thick	strange

A great many adjectives are derived from nouns:

fantasy——————▶fantastic	England——————▶English
color——————▶colorful	region——————▶regional
palace——————▶palatial	reason——————▶reasonable
America——————▶American	France——————▶French

Other adjectives are derived from verbs:

study——————▶studious	love——————▶loving
suspect——————▶suspicious	create——————▶creative
continue——————▶continuous	enjoy——————▶enjoyable

(See Chapters 3 and 4 for a discussion of how phrases and clauses can function as adjectives.)

Placement

- One-word adjectives are usually placed before the nouns they modify:

  an *important* decision   a *new* tie   a *ferocious* appetite

- Adjectives that form phrases can be placed before or after the words they modify:

  The child, *agile and more alert than others his age,* reached into the bag and found the stones.

  Agile and more alert than others his age, the child reached into the bag and found the stones.

Usage

- Use the comparative form of an adjective when comparing two people, places, or things:

  The painting on the right is the *more traditional* of the two.

- Use the superlative form of an adjective when comparing three or more people, places, or things:

  Of all the paintings in the gallery, the one by Osborne is the *most colorful.*

Adjectives of one syllable and some of two syllables form the comparative and the superlative by adding *-er* and *-est* to the base:

BASE ADJECTIVE	COMPARATIVE	SUPERLATIVE
smart	smarter	smartest
tall	taller	tallest
lucky	luckier	luckiest

The comparative *more/less* and the superlative *most/least* are used for many adjectives of two syllables and for most adjectives of three or more syllables.

BASE ADJECTIVE	COMPARATIVE	SUPERLATIVE
frequent	more/less frequent	most/least frequent
unusual	more/less unusual	most/least unusual

Irregular adjectives change their base words completely when forming the comparative and superlative:

BASE ADJECTIVE	COMPARATIVE	SUPERLATIVE
good	better	best
bad	worse	worst
many	more	most

When in doubt about the correct comparative or superlative form of an adjective, consult an unabridged dictionary.

• One-word comparative and superlative forms of adjectives should not be preceded by the word *most* or *more:*

INCORRECT	That's the *most luckiest* roll of the dice I've ever seen.
CORRECT	That's the *luckiest* roll of the dice I've ever seen.

• Some nouns can function as adjectives:

grain elevator   *senate* race
baseball glove   *dog* track
movie tickets   *state* dinner

If a noun has an adjectival form, use it when modifying other nouns:

NOT	region affairs	NOT	history landmark
BUT	regional affairs	BUT	historical landmark

• Certain adjectives are absolute in their meanings and cannot be compared. These words include *perfect, finished, dead, final, infinite,* and *ideal.*

INCORRECT	The second report is more final than the first.
CORRECT	The second report is in final form; the first is not.
INCORRECT	Robert's cake is more perfect than Larry's.
CORRECT	Robert's cake is better than Larry's.

- After linking verbs (such as *look, feel, seem,* and *appear*), use an adjective to modify the subject of the sentence:

SUBJECT	LINKING VERB	SUBJECT COMPLEMENT
Kate	looks	devilish. (adj.)
Henry	felt	pleased. (adj.)

The linking verbs in these sentences are followed by adjectives ("devilish," "pleased") that modify *Kate* and *Henry.*

- *Good* is always used as an adjective:

  Marge looks *good. (good* modifies *Marge)*
  Marge is a *good* dancer. *(good* modifies *dancer)*

- *Well* is used as an adjective after a linking verb only when it describes the subject's health:

  Marge looks *well. (well* modifies *Marge)*

ADVERBS

Adverbs modify verbs, adjectives, and other adverbs by answering such questions as "When has an action occurred?" "How?" "Where?" "How often?" "To what extent?"

Adverbs can modify verbs:

  He *aggressively* pursued a promotion.
  They wandered *aimlessly* for days.

Adverbs can modify adjectives:

  The manager submitted a *completely* reworked proposal.
  Congress has been troubled over the *rapidly* expanding budget.

Adverbs can modify other adverbs:

  The play ended *too* quickly.

Typically, adverbs are formed by adding the suffix -*ly* to an adjective:

suspicious + -ly   suspiciously   bright + -ly   brightly
affectionate + -ly affectionately strenuous + -ly strenuously
modest + -ly   modestly   obvious + -ly   obviously

Though most adverbs end in -*ly*, there are some that do not. Among them:

again   often
almost   soon
here   still
never   there
now   well

Occasionally, nouns can function as adverbs:

William will sign the lease *tomorrow*. (The adverb specifies *when* the action occurs.)

Thomas went *home*. (The adverb specifies *where* the action has occurred.)

(See Chapters 3 and 4 for a discussion of how phrases and clauses can function as adverbs.)

Placement

• Adverbs can be placed either before a verb or after its object:

Alice *regretfully* accepted the award.
Alice accepted the award *regretfully*.

(The adverb "regretfully" modifies the verb "accepted.")

• Adverbs can be placed at the beginning of a sentence, in which case they may modify the entire sentence:

Unfortunately, Alice accepted the award.

- Because a change in the placement of an adverb can result in a change of meaning, adverbs must be placed with care:

CONFUSING	Going bowling *often* leaves me with a sore arm.
	(The sentence is confusing because the adverb "often" could modify either "going bowling" or "leaves." Adverbs that can modify more than one word are called "squinting modifiers.")
IMPROVED	When I bowl often, I get a sore arm.
IMPROVED	Going bowling can often leave me with a sore arm.

Usage

- Use the comparative form of an adverb when comparing two people, places, or things:

    Leon concentrated *less intently* than Walter.

- Use the superlative form of an adverb when comparing three or more people, places, or things:

    Lisa concentrated *most intently* of them all.

- One-syllable adverbs form the comparative and the superlative by adding *-er* and *-est* to the base:

BASE ADVERB	COMPARATIVE	SUPERLATIVE
fast	faster	fastest

Adverbs of two or more syllables and adverbs ending in *-ly* use *more/less* and *most/least* for their comparative and superlative forms:

BASE ADVERB	COMPARATIVE	SUPERLATIVE
brightly	more/less brightly	most/least brightly
frequently	more/less frequently	most/least frequently
obviously	more/less obviously	most/least obviously

Irregular adverbs change their base words completely when forming the comparative and superlative:

BASE ADVERB	COMPARATIVE	SUPERLATIVE
well	better	best

When in doubt about a comparative or superlative form, consult an unabridged dictionary.

• One-word comparative and superlative forms of adverbs should not be preceded by the word *most* or *more*.

INCORRECT   The storm hit *more harder* along the coast than it did inland.

CORRECT   The storm hit *harder* along the coast than it did inland.

• The shortened forms of *slowly, quickly, loudly, sharply,* etc. are sometimes acceptable in conversation but are rarely acceptable in writing:

CONVERSATIONAL Get dressed *quick* or we'll be late.

WRITTEN   Get dressed *quickly* or we'll be late.

CONVERSATIONAL Reggie hit the ball *sharp.*

WRITTEN   Reggie hit the ball *sharply.*

• Use an adverb after linking verbs (*look, feel, seem, appear,* etc.) to modify the verb.

Henry felt poorly.

Note the difference between "Henry felt poorly" and "Henry felt poor." In the first case, "poorly" is an adverb and modifies "felt." In the second case, "poor" is an adjective and modifies Henry.

• *Well* is used as an adverb when it follows either a transitive or an intransitive verb.

Eric ran the race *well. (well* modifies *ran)*
Fran paints *well. (well* modifies *paints)*

When "well" follows a linking verb, it functions as an adjective and modifies the subject—describing its health:

Bea looks *well. (well* modifies *Bea)*

8

Verbs: Tense, Voice, and Mood

A verb establishes, or *predicates,* a relationship between a subject and the rest of a sentence.

Transitive verbs establish a relationship between the subject of the sentence and the object of the verb (the person, place, or thing that receives the action of the verb).

S	Tr V	Obj
The shopkeeper	offered	his assistance.

Intransitive verbs assert something about the subject without reference to an object.

S	Intr V
Jacob	protested.

Linking verbs, a type of intransitive verb, establish a relationship between a subject and the subject complement, which describes or renames the subject.

S	Link V	S Comp
Mr. Williams	felt	relieved.

Many verbs can be either transitive or intransitive:

Intr V	Adv		Tr V	Obj
Florence	finished	first.	Florence	finished	the race.

A verb indicates when an action has occurred (tense); whether the subject or the object of the sentence is emphasized (voice); and whether the stated action is a fact, a condition contrary to fact, or a command (mood). The ways in which you use tense, voice, and mood will determine in large measure the effectiveness of your sentences.

TENSE

The tense of a verb indicates the time at which an action or state of being occurs. There are six simple tenses in English:

PRESENT   Mrs. Simpson *calls* her son often.

PAST   Mrs. Simpson *called* her son last week.

FUTURE   Mrs. Simpson *will call* her son tomorrow.

PRESENT PERFECT   Mrs. Simpson *has called* her son once a week for years.

PAST PERFECT   Mrs. Simpson *had called* her oldest son every day for years until he told her to stop nagging him.

FUTURE PERFECT   Mrs. Simpson *will have called* her youngest son every day for twenty years on next Saturday.

All verbs change form to indicate the various tenses: some verbs are *regular* in their changes; some are *irregular*.

Regular Verbs

The six simple tenses are derived from the *principal parts* of a verb, a pattern that includes the verb's infinitive form, its past tense, and its past and present participles.

PRINCIPAL PARTS OF REGULAR VERBS

INFINITIVE	PAST TENSE	PRESENT PARTICIPLE	PAST PARTICIPLE
(to) walk	walked	(am, are, is) walking	(have, has, had) walked
(to) play	played	(am, are, is) playing	(have, has, had) played
(to) call	called	(am, are, is) calling	(have, has, had) called

As you can see, the past tense of a regular verb is formed by adding -ed to the infinitive. The past participle is also formed in this way but is always used with the auxiliary have, has, or had. The perfect tenses are all formed with the past participle:

PRESENT PERFECT Lorenzo has finished the sculpture.
PAST PERFECT Lorenzo had finished the sculpture.
FUTURE PERFECT Lorenzo will have finished the sculpture.

Even though the past participle and past tense forms are identical for regular verbs (e.g., "called"), the meanings of sentences in which they appear differ:

PAST TENSE FORM Willard called the pizza parlor yesterday.
PAST PARTICIPLE Willard has called the pizza parlor.

The two tenses indicate that the action in these sentences has occurred at differing times. In the first instance, the action has been completed at a definite time in the past. In the second instance, the action has been completed at an indefinite time.

Irregular Verbs

Take special care to learn the principal parts of irregular verbs, whose past tense and past participle are not formed by adding -ed to the verb stem. A complete list of irregular verbs is far too long to include here. A few examples follow:

PRINCIPAL PARTS OF IRREGULAR VERBS

INFINITIVE	PAST TENSE	PAST PARTICIPLE
(to) ring	rang	(have, has, had) rung
(to) rise	rose	(have, has, had) risen
(to) grow	grew	(have, has, had) grown
(to) drive	drove	(have, has, had) driven
(to) drink	drank	(have, has, had) drunk
(to) eat	ate	(have, has, had) eaten

Perhaps the most troublesome irregular verb is also the one used most often: *to be.* You should memorize its conjugation:

FIRST PERSON

	SINGULAR	PLURAL
PRESENT TENSE	I am	we are
PAST TENSE	I was	we were
FUTURE	I will be	we will be
PRESENT PERFECT	I have been	we have been
PAST PERFECT	I had been	we had been
FUTURE PERFECT	I will have been	we will have been

SECOND PERSON

	SINGULAR AND PLURAL
PRESENT TENSE	you are
PAST TENSE	you were
FUTURE	you will be
PRESENT PERFECT	you have been
PAST PERFECT	you had been
FUTURE PERFECT	you will have been

THIRD PERSON

	SINGULAR	PLURAL
PRESENT TENSE	he is, she is, it is	they are
PAST TENSE	he was, she was it was	they were
FUTURE	he will be she will be, it will be	they will be
PRESENT PERFECT	he has been she has been	they have been
PAST PERFECT	he had been she had been	they had been
FUTURE PERFECT	he will have been	they will have been

When in doubt as to which principal part of a verb is joined with the auxiliary *has, had,* or *have,* consult a dictionary. Most entries are introduced as follows:

draw (drô) *v.* **drew (droo), drawn, drawing, draws. —***tr.*

The first word that you see in boldface is the infinitive form of the verb *(draw).* The next boldface word (after the phonetic spelling and the designation that the word is a verb [*v.*]) is the past tense form of the verb *(drew);* and the next word is the past participle *(drawn).* Next are two other forms of the verb: the present participle *(drawing)* and the third person singular present tense *(draws).* The abbreviations *tr.* and *intr.* indicate whether, or under what conditions, a verb is transitive and intransitive (see pages 19–20.)

Present Tense

[Infinitive form of verb: *to believe*]

	SINGULAR	PLURAL
FIRST PERSON	I *believe*	we *believe*
SECOND PERSON	you *believe*	you *believe*
THIRD PERSON	he *believes* she *believes*	they *believe*

The infinitive form of a verb (without the word *to*) is used as the present tense in all cases other than the third person singular. When a verb follows *he, she,* or *it* (or a noun that can be substituted for one of these), the present tense is formed by adding the letter *s* to its infinitive form.

Robert (he) *draws* whenever he gets the opportunity.
Robert and Sara (they) *draw* whenever they get the opportunity.

USES OF THE PRESENT TENSE
• The present tense is used to indicate an action occurring in the present time:

Watch as the artist *draws* his picture.

• The present tense can denote an action occurring in the future:

> Tomorrow, he *draws* the Statue of Liberty.

(More often, the future tense is indicated by the auxiliary *will.*)

• The present tense can be used to show an already completed action, especially when the reference is to a book, article, or report:

> In his *Annual Report,* the chairman of the board *draws* a troubling analogy between our company and a man lost at sea.

• The present tense can be used to indicate a repeated action:

> Every morning, beginning at six o'clock, Lauren *draws* for an hour.

Past Tense

[Infinitive form of verb: *to sneeze*]

	SINGULAR	PLURAL
FIRST PERSON	I *sneezed*	we *sneezed*
SECOND PERSON	you *sneezed*	you *sneezed*
THIRD PERSON	he *sneezed* she *sneezed*	they *sneezed*

The past tense of a verb indicates an action completed at some definite time in the past. This tense retains the same form for all three persons, both in the singular and in the plural. Form the past tense of a regular verb by adding -ed to its infinitive. Irregular verbs expressed in the past tense do not follow a simple pattern. (For example: go/went, take/took.) When in doubt about the past tense form of a verb, consult a dictionary.

> Lauren (she) *visited* Mount Rushmore.
> Lauren and Rafe (they) *went* to the foot of the cliffs.

Future Tense

[Infinitive form of verb: *to attend*]

	SINGULAR	PLURAL
FIRST PERSON	I *will attend*	we *will attend*
	OR	OR
	I *shall attend*	we *shall attend*
SECOND PERSON	you *will attend*	you *will attend*
THIRD PERSON	he *will attend* she *will attend*	they *will attend*

The future tense is used to denote an action or a state of being that will occur in the future. This tense is formed by combining the infinitive form of the verb with the auxiliary *shall* or *will*. Some grammarians insist that the auxiliary *shall* is used correctly only with the first person pronouns *I* and *we*, as in "I shall attend the meeting" and "We shall attend the game." The auxiliary *will*, according to this view, is used with the second and third persons. However, the distinction is quickly disappearing and for most occasions *shall* and *will* may be used interchangeably for the first person—*shall* being the more formal of the two auxiliaries.

FORMAL   I *shall speak* to the boss in the morning.
LESS FORMAL   I *will speak* to the boss in the morning.

Present Perfect Tense

[Infinitive form of verb: *to go*]

	SINGULAR	PLURAL
FIRST PERSON	I *have gone*	we *have gone*
SECOND PERSON	you *have gone*	you *have gone*
THIRD PERSON	he *has gone* she *has gone*	they *have gone*

The present perfect tense indicates an action either completed at some indefinite time in the past or begun in the past and continuing into the present. This tense is formed by joining the auxiliary *have* or *has* to the past participle of a verb. (Note that *has* follows only the third person singular noun or pronoun.)

As part of his legal work, Stephen *has researched* deeds at the county courthouse.

For the past year, Mr. and Mrs. Wilson *have considered* moving to Peru.

Past Perfect Tense

[Infinitive form of verb: *to tell*]

	SINGULAR	PLURAL
FIRST PERSON	I *had told*	we *had told*
SECOND PERSON	you *had told*	you *had told*
THIRD PERSON	he *had told* she *had told*	they *had told*

The past perfect tense denotes an action that has occurred in the past prior to some other action. This tense is formed by joining the auxiliary *had* to the past participle of the verb.

Before the decision was announced, Henry *had considered* withdrawing his name from the ballot.

Note on Usage: In using the past perfect tense, remember to sequence events within the sentence properly: clearly establish a simple past tense (or an event that has taken place at some fixed time in the past) before using a past perfect tense.

Before electricity came to Mason County, in 1945, residents *had lived* by candle and kerosene light.

("Before electricity came, in 1945," establishes a definite time in the past.)

Future Perfect Tense

[Infinitive form of verb: *to travel*]

	SINGULAR	PLURAL
FIRST PERSON	I *will have traveled*	we *will have traveled*
	OR	OR
	I *shall have traveled*	we *shall have traveled*
SECOND PERSON	you *will have traveled*	you *will have traveled*
THIRD PERSON	he *will have traveled* she *will have traveled*	they *will have traveled*

The future perfect tense denotes an action that occurs in the future prior to some other action. This tense is formed by joining the auxiliary *shall have* or *will have* to the past participle of a verb. (See page 102 regarding the use of *shall* and *will.*)

> Before the meeting this afternoon, I *will have spoken* to all the interested parties.

Note on Usage: In using the future perfect tense, remember to sequence events within a sentence properly: clearly establish a simple future tense (or an event that is to take place at some fixed time in the future) before using a future perfect tense.

> I *will have completed* the report in time for the next meeting.

("The next meeting" establishes a definite time in the future.)

Progressive Tenses

The progressive tenses are formed by joining the verb *to be* with the present participle (the *-ing* form) of a verb. The progressive tenses indicate an ongoing action, whether it occurs in the present, past, or future:

PRESENT PROGRESSIVE	Eric *is walking* home.
PAST PROGRESSIVE	Eric *was walking* home.
FUTURE PROGRESSIVE	Eric *will be walking* home.
PRESENT PERFECT PROGRESSIVE	Eric *has been walking* home from work for years.
PAST PERFECT PROGRESSIVE	Eric *had been walking* home from work regularly, until he developed a back problem.
FUTURE PERFECT PROGRESSIVE	Eric *will have been walking* home for a month on next Tuesday.

Auxiliaries

must	can	could	should
would	may	did/does	has/have/had
might	will	shall	is/are/was/were/been
ought			

Auxiliary verbs help establish the relationship between a subject and the rest of a sentence. A form of the auxiliary *to do* establishes the tense of a verb:

PRESENT   He does cry occasionally.
PAST   He did cry occasionally.

Most auxiliaries, however, do not indicate tense. Their function is to add other types of information to a sentence, answering such questions as—Will the verb express an obligation felt by the subject? a sense of urgency? a comment on the likelihood of an event's happening? Auxiliaries account for the difference in meaning between "She must go," "She might go," and "She ought to go."

VOICE

Voice is a term that indicates whether a writer has emphasized the *doer* or the *receiver* of an action.

Active Voice

When you wish to emphasize the *doer* of an action, use an active-voice verb:

The counselor *had won* the case.
The flight instructor *committed* a grievous error.

Passive Voice

When you wish to emphasize the *receiver* of an action, use a passive-voice verb:*

The case *had been won* by the counselor.
A grievous error *was committed* by the flight instructor.

*I owe this distinction between the active and passive voices—between performing and receiving the action of a verb—to Hulon Willis, *Modern Descriptive English Grammar* (San Francisco: Chandler Publishing, 1972), p. 179.

To change a sentence from the active voice to the passive voice, follow these steps:

1. Begin with a sentence that has a transitive verb expressed in the active voice.

   The flight instructor committed a grievous error.

2. Switch the order of the subject and direct object.

   a grievous error committed the flight instructor

3. Add a form of "to be" directly before the verb, and add the preposition "by" directly after the verb.

   A grievous error *was* committed *by* the flight instructor.

4. (Optional) Delete the prepositional phrase from the new sentence:

   A grievous error was committed.

Note the difference in meaning and structure between the following groups of sentences:

ACTIVE	Babe Ruth hit the ball.
PASSIVE	The ball was hit by Babe Ruth.
	OR
	The ball was hit.
ACTIVE	Lincoln wrote "The Gettysburg Address."
PASSIVE	"The Gettysburg Address" was written by Lincoln.
ACTIVE	The researcher placed the petri dish in a warm oven.
PASSIVE	The petri dish was placed in a warm oven by the researcher.
	OR
	The petri dish was placed in a warm oven.

Using the Active and Passive Voices

The passive voice is less direct and less forceful than the active. Use the passive voice only when you wish to avoid a redundant subject, to remove from the sentence an awkward reference to yourself, or to create an impression of scientific or technical objectivity. In the sentence pairs below, the passive construction is preferable to the active.

Avoid a redundant subject by using the passive voice:

ACTIVE   Horse breeders raise a great many horses in Maryland.

PASSIVE   A great many horses are raised in Maryland.

(The unnecessary phrase "by horse breeders" has been deleted from the end of the sentence.)

Avoid an awkward subject by using the passive voice:

ACTIVE   I discuss the migratory patterns of hummingbirds in this book.

PASSIVE   The migratory patterns of hummingbirds are discussed in this book.

(The implied phrase "by me" is deleted from the end of the sentence.)

Create an impression of scientific or technical objectivity by using the passive voice:

ACTIVE   I recommend that you test the wires to assure a complete circuit.

PASSIVE   It is recommended that you test the wires to assure a complete circuit.

(The implied phrase "by me" is deleted after the word "recommended.")

MOOD

There are three moods in spoken and written English, each of which indicates how a speaker or writer regards the action of the sentence.

Indicative Mood

The indicative mood of a verb indicates a statement of fact (or what is believed to be fact). Most of what we write and speak is expressed in the indicative mood:

> Bats leave their caves at dusk and return at dawn.
> Gold was valued by the ancients because it resembled the sun.

Imperative Mood

The imperative mood expresses a command or direction. The subject of an imperative sentence is not usually stated but is understood to be "you":

> Pull the rip cord at the count of three.
> Do not panic if the parachute fails to open.

Subjunctive Mood

The subjunctive mood expresses doubt, urgency, desirability, a wish, a recommendation, a condition contrary to fact, an unlikely condition, and related concepts:

> If *I were* home, I would be playing the piano.
> We request that *she attend* the meeting.

Note that when using the subjunctive mood for the first and the third person singular, you have an apparent disagreement in number between subjects and verbs (i.e., *I were, she attend*). However, with the second person singular and the plural conjugations in the subjunctive mood, there is no apparent disagreement:

SECOND PERSON SINGULAR   If *you were* independently wealthy, would you work forty hours a week?

THIRD PERSON PLURAL   We request that *they perform* their juggling routine.

The subjunctive mood is expressed most often in four sentence structures:

1. The "if" statement:

   If he were on vacation, he would be sipping lemonade and reading *Wuthering Heights*.

(In the first clause, a condition contrary to fact is established; in the second clause, the auxiliary "would," "might," or "could" is used.)

2. The "as if" statement:

   Beth stocks her pantry *as if she were* expecting a calamity.
   She laughs *as though she were* a child of three.

(In this construction, the "as if" or "as though" clause follows the main clause of the sentence.)

3. The "request" statement—The subjunctive mood is used in sentences containing the verbs *request, recommend, urge, believe, desire,* and *doubt,* followed by a clause beginning with *that:*

   I recommend that *he be* present at his own trial.
   She urged that *he wait* for a taxi.

4. The simple statement with selected auxiliaries—The verb in the subjunctive mood may be preceded by the auxiliary *should, ought to, must, might, could,* or *may:*

   He should not *refuse*.
   She must *reconsider*.
   He ought to *attend*.
   May *you be* healthy for a hundred years.

Agreement Between Subject and Verb, Pronoun and Antecedent

SUBJECT/VERB AGREEMENT

Subjects and verbs agree with one another in number and person.

Number is a term indicating whether a subject or verb is singular or plural:

SINGULAR	Zanuck <u>rows</u> along the Erie canal every morning.
PLURAL	<u>His sister Zelda and her husband Zabar</u> usually <u>wait</u> for his return before driving to work.

Person is a term that indicates whether the subject is the one speaking—first person; the one spoken to—second person; or the one spoken about—third person.

FIRST PERSON	<u>I walk</u> to the store.
SECOND PERSON	<u>You drive</u> to the store.
THIRD PERSON	<u>Wilson flies</u> to the store.

Present tense verbs end with *s* when following a singular subject in the third person:

I *admire* Mary.
Fred *admires* Bette.
Mary and Bette *admire* Joe.

I *wander* alone at night.
He *wanders* through the garden.
They *wander* along the seashore.

The ending of a past tense verb remains the same, regardless of the number and person of the subject:

I *ate* a ginger snap.
Mr. Hollins *ate* his sandwich.
Mr. and Mrs. Hollins *ate* Peking duck.
I *remained* awake.
He *remained* awake.
They both *remained* awake.

Subject/verb agreement does not usually pose a problem when a subject is easily identified with regard to person and number. However, when a phrase separates a subject from its verb, or when it is unclear whether a subject is singular or plural, subject/verb agreement can be troublesome. Follow the guidelines below when in doubt about the agreement between subject and verb.

Determining the Number of a Subject

• The predicate verb of a sentence always agrees in number with its subject, not with any of the words in an intervening phrase or clause:

The musicians at the studio are professionals.

Chicago's inland seaport, the largest in the world, is situated on Lake Michigan.

Chicago, which has the largest of the world's inland seaports, is situated on Lake Michigan.

Mr. Eliot, who is expected to arrive at Penn Station with several reporters, regards his farewell speech as the most important of his career.

• A linking verb—like all verbs—agrees in number with its subject. Avoid the temptation to make a linking verb agree with the subject complement.

S	Link V	S Comp
His extraordinary talents	are	the cause of his success.
The cause of his success	is	his extraordinary talents.

- A subject joined by the conjunction *and* is plural in meaning when that subject specifies two or more persons, places, or things:

> A dog and a baseball glove are no longer a boy's best friends.
>
> Reporters and their editors insist on the journalist's right not to divulge sources of information.
>
> The foreman and the manager have decided to leave production quotas up to the employees.

(The foreman and the manager are not the same person.)

- A subject joined by the conjunction *and* is singular in number when that subject specifies one person, place, or thing:

> The foreman and manager has decided to leave production quotas up to the employees.

(One person is both foreman and manager.)

- A subject joined by the conjunction *or* or *nor* is considered singular when the individual parts of the subject are singular:

> An engine tune-up or a brake replacement costs well over one hundred dollars for most cars.

A subject joined by *or* or *nor* is considered plural when the individual parts of the subject are plural:

> Neither children nor their parents enjoy family disputes.

Sometimes one part of a subject joined by *or* or *nor* is singular and the other part is plural. In that case the verb agrees in number with the part closest to the verb:

> Either the tide or the high winds are responsible for the damage along the shore.
>
> Either the high winds or the tide is responsible for the damage along the shore.

• A collective noun—such as *group, family, team, audience,* and *staff*—is considered singular or plural, depending on its sense in the sentence.

The staff is loyal to its director.

(The subject has a singular sense. "The staff" functions as a unit.)

The staff are ill-at-ease, and some wish to resign.

(The subject has a plural sense. "The staff" functions as a collection of individuals.)

Many writers consider the plural use of "staff" and other collective nouns to be awkward; you can avoid this awkwardness by adding a plural noun to the sentence:

The staff members are ill-at-ease.

• A gerund or an infinitive phrase that functions as the subject of a sentence is regarded as singular in number. Such phrases are often followed by the third person singular form of *to be: is.*

Driving in the city at rush hour is a challenge.
To be chosen as a congressional page is an honor.

• In sentences beginning with an expletive, the verb agrees with the subject of the sentence, not the expletive.

SENTENCE WITH EXPLETIVE: There are fifty protesters gathered in front of the courthouse.

SENTENCE ORDER REVERSED: Fifty protesters are gathered in front of the courthouse.

• Nouns that are plural in form but singular in meaning—such as *news, physics, mathematics, economics, politics,* and *gymnastics* —require a singular verb.

News travels quickly in small towns.
Mathematics is a field of study that comes easily to some and painfully to others.

Politics, athletics, genetics, and other nouns ending with "ics" can be singular or plural in meaning. When the noun refers to an organized activity, it takes a singular verb; when the noun refers to the activities of individuals within a group or to varied activities, the noun takes a plural verb:

> Politics is not an activity for the faint of heart.
> Their politics are unexpectedly diverse, considering that each member of the family works in the same business and belongs to the same social groups.

• The indefinite pronouns *every, each, anybody, no one, none,* and *another* are regarded as singular:

> Each of the children has settled far from home.
> No one hears from them anymore.

The indefinite pronouns *ones* and *others* are regarded as plural:

> The others are on their way.

The indefinite pronouns *all, some, few,* and *most* can be either singular or plural, depending on their meaning in a sentence:

> A few is all he could manage.
> Few have the qualifications to become astronauts.

• Titles of books, stories, articles, plays, movies, etc. are regarded as singular, even though words in the title may be plural:

> Tender Mercies is a film worth seeing.
> "In Dreams Begin Responsibilities" is a story by Delmore Schwartz.

• Individual words that are italicized and referred to as words are considered singular:

> Hippopotami is the plural form of hippopotamus.
> Martin Luther King's "I have a dream" is a phrase that has inspired millions of people.

• Numbers, sums of money, and units of time are considered to be singular in number:

<u>One million dollars</u> <u>*is*</u> a healthy return on a fifty-cent lottery ticket. <u>Three weeks</u> <u>seems</u> like a long time to convalesce from a sore throat.

Agreement Between Subjects and Auxiliary Verbs

Only three auxiliary verbs change form according to the person and number of the subject: *to be, to do,* and *to have.* When these verbs function as auxiliaries, they change form; the second, main part of the verb remains the same.

to be	I *am* going to sleep.
	He *is* going to sleep.
	We *are* going to sleep.
to do	I *do* take vitamins.
	He *does* take vitamins.
to have	I *have* been home.
	He *has* been home.

Other auxiliary verbs retain their form for first, second, and third persons and for singular and plural subjects.

I *might* be going.	We *might* be going.
You *might* be going.	They *might* be going.
He *might* be going.	

PRONOUN/ANTECEDENT AGREEMENT

A pronoun agrees with its antecedent (the word or words that the pronoun renames) in three respects: person, number, and gender (male, female, neuter). Determining the gender and person of an antecedent is seldom a problem. The context of a sentence will usually make clear the distinctions between male and female and among the first, second, and third persons. What can be troublesome, though, is determining the number of the antecedent—the same concern as when you want to make a verb agree with its subject. The following rules should help clarify when antecedents are singular and when they are plural.

Determining the Number of an Antecedent

• An antecedent joined by the conjunction *and* can be singular or plural, depending on its sense in the sentence. When it refers to two or more persons, places, or things, an antecedent is plural in number and should be followed by a plural pronoun. When *and* joins two antecedents that refer to the same person, place, or thing, the antecedent is considered singular in number and should be followed by a singular pronoun:

>PLURAL ANTECEDENT: *Roy and Dale* rode *their* horses into the sunset.
>
>SINGULAR ANTECEDENT: *The foreman and manager* decided to leave the comfort of *his* office in order to be with the workers on the assembly line.

(One person is both foreman and manager.)

• A collective noun (such as *group, family, team, audience, staff,* and *class*) can be singular or plural, depending on its sense in a sentence. A collective noun with a singular sense should be followed by a singular pronoun; a collective noun with a plural sense should be followed by a plural pronoun:

>SINGULAR: The *staff* is loyal to *its* director.
>
>PLURAL: The *staff* are being forced from *their* positions as the new administration takes office.

• Antecedents joined by the conjunctions *either/or, neither/nor,* and *or* are considered singular in number when the word or phrase following the conjunction is singular. These antecedents should be followed by a singular pronoun.

>Either *Ronald* or *Michael* will bring *his* radio.
>
>Either *the state governments* or *the Federal Highway Commission* would have to declare *its* support for the new interstate road system before construction could begin.

• Antecedents joined by the conjunctions *either/or, neither/nor,* or *or* are considered plural in number when the word or phrase following the conjunction is plural. These antecedents should be followed by a plural pronoun.

> Neither *the senators* nor *the congressmen* from Alabama, Texas, and California were willing to cast *their* votes for the bill to raise taxes.

> Either *the Federal Highway Commission* or *the state governments* would have to declare *their* support for the new interstate road system before construction could begin.

• Antecedents that are indefinite pronouns—such as *every, each, anybody, somebody, no one, none*—are usually regarded as singular in number and take a singular pronoun.

> *Somebody* left *his* coat on the sofa.

> *No one* in *her* right mind would go into that house after midnight.

Note: The context of a sentence or paragraph may clearly establish whether an indefinite antecedent is exclusively male or female, so that selecting the appropriate pronoun for agreement poses no problem.

> After the Freemasons' meeting, *someone* left *his* hat in the hall.

> As the meeting of the League of Women Voters was beginning, *someone* raised *her* hand to make a statement.

• When choosing the gender of a pronoun that refers to an antecedent not clearly masculine or feminine, you have several options for wording:

ACCEPTABLE	Each should give according to *her* ability.
ACCEPTABLE	Each should give according to *his* ability.
WORDY	Each should give according to *his* or *her* ability.
UNGRAMMATICAL	Each should give according to *their* abilities.

Note: Once you have decided on the number and gender of an antecedent, remain consistent in your subsequent use of pronouns. (Some writers, in an attempt to be evenhanded, alternate their use of pronouns in such cases—sometimes using the masculine forms, other times using the feminine forms.)

NOT   Each of them is willing to risk *her* freedom for what *they* believe.

BUT   Each of them is willing to risk *her* freedom for what *she* believes.

- Demonstrative pronouns should agree in number with the nouns that follow them. *This* and *that* are singular in number; *these* and *those* are plural:

This job is difficult.
These bricks are heavy.
That sculpture is inspiring.
Those artichokes are delicious.

- Demonstrative pronouns should also agree in number with the words *kind, sort, type, brand,* etc.:

this kind of question   *that* type of motor
these brands of paint   *those* sorts of desserts

- A relative pronoun (*who, that,* etc.) has the same number as the noun it renames. Verbs within a relative clause agree in number with the relative pronoun.

The people who are waving flags call themselves patriots.

(The relative pronoun *who* renames the plural subject *people.* Both the predicate verb *call* and the verb in the relative clause, *are waving,* are plural and agree in number with the subject.)

Mr. Farrar, who is a concert violinist, was born in Memphis.

(The relative pronoun *who* renames the singular subject *Mr. Farrar.* Both the predicate verb *was born* and the verb in the relative clause, *is,* are singular and agree in number with the subject.)

PART THREE

Punctuation/Mechanics

10

Punctuation

Marks of punctuation—commas, periods, etc.—help readers to interpret sentences. Some marks are obligatory, required to prevent misreading; many other marks are optional and depend on the particular emphasis a writer wishes to give. For instance, ending a sentence with an exclamation point, rather than a period, or using parentheses instead of a pair of commas or dashes, determines how a sentence is read and understood.

Because judgment plays so important a role in the placement of many punctuation marks, the rules provided below are occasionally violated by experienced writers. However, before any rule is violated, one should first know the rule in question and then be aware, based on the needs of a particular sentence, why an alternate method of punctuation is desirable.

COMMA

The comma is a mark of punctuation used to group and separate words within a sentence. When read, the comma indicates a pause.

- Long introductory phrases and introductory dependent clauses that function as modifiers are followed by a comma. For short introductory phrases and dependent clauses, the use of a comma is optional. Always use a comma after two or more phrases that introduce a sentence:

> Gently lifting the window, the detective slipped into the room.
>
> At sixteen, Judy Garland was a well-known actress.
> OR
> At sixteen Judy Garland was a well-known actress.
>
> When man began to settle in villages about 10,000 years ago, he had to clear the land in order to raise domesticated animals.

Exception: When a phrase or clause serves as the subject of a sentence, *do not* put a comma between it and the predicate:

> *To be informed* is not an easy task when everyone about you is confused.
>
> *Overstretching of muscles and tendons* can lead to tears and strains.

• Place a comma before the final phrase or clause of a sentence when these establish a contrast, an exception, or a qualification:

> Nature lovers who take long walks at sunset should spray themselves with insect repellent, unless they aren't concerned about marauding flies and mosquitoes.
>
> The Pilgrims landed in Massachusetts, not in Florida.

• Phrases and clauses in the middle of a sentence are set off by a pair of commas if they are not essential to the sentence's meaning. If phrases or clauses are essential, do not set them off. (See page 88 for a discussion of essential and nonessential clauses.)

> NONESSENTIAL
>
> The best route, *I believe*, from New York to Washington takes you through Paris and Madrid.
>
> Annapolis, *which is the capital of Maryland*, is also the home of the U.S. Naval Academy.

ESSENTIAL

The desire *to work a forty-hour week in four days* is not a new one. Books *that are made with acid-free paper* are expensive but durable.

• Place a comma before a coordinate conjunction if it separates two independent clauses:

Fashion designers have a financial interest in changing styles every season, for a world of consistent tastes in clothing would put many out of business.

Clothing design is the most exciting and least disruptive barometer of a nation's mood, so I am surprised by some people's attacks on the industry.

Exception: DO NOT place a comma before a coordinate conjunction that joins two verbs:

The Seeing Eye dog *looked* both ways and then *crossed* the street.

• Use *a pair of commas* to set off a parallel construction that repeats and extends some sentence element. Use one comma and a period if the construction ends the sentence.

The childhood I remember so well, the childhood of private passions and restlessness, remains an important key to my personality.

I never wanted to live too far from the big woods, too far from the network of trails and streams that led north through the glaciated country of Minnesota.   HARRISON E. SALISBURY

• Use *a pair of commas* to set off transitional expressions or adverbial conjunctions (see page 15) that occur in the middle of a sentence:

The speaker's conclusion, unfortunately, did not follow from his arguments.

Mrs. Rourke agreed, therefore, that the best course of action would be to wait six weeks before introducing her new product.

Exception: Writers sometimes choose not to place commas around the adverbial conjunction *therefore* when it immediately follows the subject of a sentence:

> Mrs. Rourke therefore agreed that the best course of action would be to wait six weeks before introducing her new product.

• When an adverbial conjunction introduces a sentence, punctuate it in one of two ways:

Conclude the previous sentence with a period, and capitalize the first word of the adverbial conjunction. Place a comma after the conjunction:

> The purpose of the Voting Rights Act was to ensure that all eligible citizens would have the opportunity to vote. *However,* the results of our most recent national elections indicate that large numbers of Americans either are not registered or do not care to cast their ballots.

Conclude the previous sentence with a semicolon, and place a comma after the adverbial conjunction:

> The purpose of the Voting Rights Act was to ensure that all eligible citizens would have the opportunity to vote; *however,* the results of our most recent national elections indicate that large numbers of Americans either are not registered or do not care to cast their ballots.

• Use a comma to set off an absolute phrase (see pages 46–47) that begins or ends a sentence:

> *Her mission completed,* the botanist returned to the base camp.
> The pilot squinted, *his eyes hurting from the flash of the explosion.*

• Use a comma to set off questions within a sentence:

> The market is at the corner, isn't it?
> The President returned from California, didn't he?

• Use commas to separate a series of three or more items:

> Cupboards, linen presses, wardrobes, and other large storage

pieces were a necessity in American homes until the innovation of built-in closets and pantries in the late 19th century.

WILLIAM C. KETCHUM, JR.

Exceptions:

1. Writers sometimes choose not to place a comma between the final two elements of a series:

   Remember to get flour, sugar and walnuts.

   Some grammarians object when this final comma is omitted; so the safest course, therefore, is to use the final comma, since a sentence will never be considered incorrectly punctuated if you do so.

2. When *coordinate conjunctions* join the items of a series, do not use commas to separate items:

   I could swim and fish and hike.

• Place a comma between *coordinate adjectives,* adjectives that modify a single word but are not joined by the conjunction "and."

   The garrulous, gentle widow made friends easily.

Note: Do not place a comma between a pair or a series of adjectives that do not modify the same word. (A test you can use: Place "and" between the adjectives. If the result is awkward, do not use a comma.)

   A bright red car calls attention to itself.

(The adjective "bright" modifies "red," not "car." Compare with the example above, where "garrulous" and "gentle" both modify "widow.")

• Use a comma to mark the omission of one or two words in a balanced sentence:

   Some explorers seek adventure to make names for themselves; others, to reach beyond the boundaries of the known.

("Others" is substituted for the words "other explorers seek adventure.")

• Use a comma to set off a noun in direct address that occurs at the beginning or end of a sentence. If this noun appears in the middle of the sentence, use a pair of commas:

> Mark, please don't finish the potato chips.
> I asked you not to finish the potato chips, Mark.
> I can't tell, Mark, if you're listening.

• Use a comma to set off an introductory remark (such as *of course, yes, indeed, to be sure, obviously*) from the rest of a sentence:

> Indeed, Miss Grumman was so popular that her studio hired bodyguards to protect her from the crush of adoring fans.

Exception: *Maybe, perhaps,* and other introductory remarks that do not break the flow of a sentence should not be followed by commas:

> Perhaps she should retire from show business.

• Use a comma following the expressions *namely, for example (e.g.), that is (i.e.), for instance, especially,* and so on:

> Dozens of childhood stars have suffered from identifying too strongly with the roles they've played; for instance, Frances Deavers, believing herself to be the angel she portrayed in *Heaven's Trumpet,* jumped from a warehouse roof and fractured her arm.

• Use a comma to introduce a quotation or to complete a quotation that does not conclude a sentence. Commas and periods are placed *inside* quotation marks.

> Grumman's producer said, "It's brutal out there."
> "But I really don't mind the attention," she replied.

Note: Commas should not be used to introduce indirect quotations:

> Susan Grumman answered that she would live as she pleased.

• Use a comma in place of an exclamation point when the exclamatory remark is a mild one:

> Well, I don't mind.

• Use commas in correspondence according to conventions for names, titles, addresses, and dates.

1. When an address is written in block form:

—place a comma after a name if it is followed by a title (and between titles if more than one is used).

—place a comma between a city (or county) and its state.

—DO NOT place a comma between a state and its zip code.

Mr. Richard Greene, Manager
The Carpet Clearinghouse
1309 Franklin Avenue
Hamilton, New York 10167

2. Place a comma between the day of the month and the year. No comma is needed between the month and the year if the date is omitted:

August 12, 1985   August 1985

Two other conventions are accepted. The second form is used most often when writing invitations.

12 August 1983
the twelfth of August, 1983

If you include the day of the week in a date, place a comma between the day and the month:

Linda arrived on Monday, August 12, 1985.

3. When writing out an address in a sentence, place a comma after each self-contained item of information:

Send the letter to Dr. Ron Evans, Staff Psychologist, Shelbourne Hospital, 241 Hanover Street, Wheaton, Maryland 21063.

• Use commas in numbers that have four or more digits: Some writers prefer to omit the comma in a four-digit number that is a multiple of fifty:

2,106,427   106,427   6,427   3500   3350   1050

Exceptions: Commas are omitted in page numbers, street numbers, and phone numbers:

page 2051   dial 664-7291   2701 Rockwood Avenue

SEMICOLON

The semicolon signals a pause longer than a comma but briefer than a period.

• Place a semicolon after the first independent clause of a lengthy compound sentence when one or both of the clauses contain commas. Place a comma—rather than a semicolon—after the first independent clause if there is little chance of misinterpreting the sentence.

> The format you choose for a résumé should reflect your personal needs; so consider your qualifications, your objective, your work history, and the kind of employer you seek, before you select a style.

> Fashion designers have a financial interest in changing styles every season, for without the prospect of raised or lowered hemlines, they'd soon be out of work.

For emphasis, use a semicolon to separate independent clauses of a lengthy compound sentence even when commas do not appear in either clause:

> He who gives himself entirely to his fellow-men appears to them useless and selfish; but he who gives himself partially to them is pronounced a benefactor and philanthropist.
>
> HENRY DAVID THOREAU

• Substitute a semicolon for the comma and coordinate conjunction that normally join two independent clauses:

> We have abolished space here on the little earth; we can never abolish the space that yawns between the stars.
>
> ARTHUR C. CLARKE

In the Middle Ages the ladder of promotion was through the Church; there was no other way for a clever, poor boy to go up.

J. BRONOWSKI

Note: In fiction and essay writing, short and balanced compound sentences are sometimes separated by commas (and not semicolons):

Beverly complained of this, she worried about it, she was proud of it.   JOYCE CAROL OATES

• Place a semicolon before an adverbial conjunction (see pages 33–35) that joins two independent clauses:

A new computer salesman receives some thirteen months of education, including classroom instruction, computer-aided study, and on-the-job training with senior salesmen; *afterward*, each man spends about three weeks a year learning updated computer applications and selling techniques.   KATHERINE DAVIS FISHMAN

• Place semicolons between items in a series when the items contain punctuation and/or when they are especially long:

Copies of the agreement should be sent to Robert White in Albany, New York; to Francis DeLorean in Miami, Florida; and to Lawrence Heffernan in Quincy, Massachusetts.

Of the seven children, all told, that had been born to them, three had died; one girl had gone to Kansas; one boy had gone to Sioux Falls, never even to be heard of after; another boy had gone to Washington; and the last girl lived five counties away in the same state, but was so burdened with cares of her own that she rarely gave them a thought.   THEODORE DREISER

• Place a semicolon before an *appositive phrase* introduced by expressions such as *that is, for example, namely,* and *especially:*

I was in too deep; that is, too deep for me to be risking revelations to so new a friend, though not clear beyond my depth, as I looked at it.   MARK TWAIN

• Place a semicolon outside of quotation marks when it is not part of the quoted material:

> I heartily accept the motto—"That government is best which governs least"; and I should like to see it acted up to more rapidly and systematically.   HENRY DAVID THOREAU

COLON

The colon signals an emphatic pause within a sentence— longer than a semicolon but briefer than a period.

• Use a colon to introduce a series. When the series is presented in sentence form, do not capitalize the items unless they are proper nouns:

> Several supplies should be included in everyone's backpack for hiking: matches, a mirror for signaling, two compasses, and two copies of every map.

When a series is presented in list form, capitalize the first letter of each item if it is introduced by a number or letter. If introduced by a dash, the first letter may remain in lower case:

> Several supplies should be included in everyone's backpack for hiking:
>
> | 1. Matches | OR | —matches |
> | 2. A mirror for signaling | | —a mirror for signaling |
> | 3. Two compasses | | —two compasses |
> | 4. Two copies of every map | | —two copies of every map |

Note: The items in a series should be grammatically parallel. See page 189.

• Use a colon before an appositive that ends a sentence. The first letter of the appositive, if it is a sentence, may be capitalized (though some writers choose not to).

There are today a few remaining large reptiles on Earth, the most striking of which is the Komodo dragon of Indonesia: cold-blooded, not very bright, but a predator exhibiting a chilling fixity of purpose.   CARL SAGAN

• Use a colon after "the following" or "as follows":

The colon is used in the following ways: to distinguish between titles and subtitles and to introduce a series, an appositive phrase, or a quotation.

• Use a colon to introduce long or formal quotations:

The farmer, poet, and essayist Wendell Berry has written: "Though as a man I inherit great evils and the possibility of great loss and suffering, I know that my life is blessed and graced by the yearly flowering of the bluebells."

• Use the colon to distinguish hours from minutes and the numbers in a ratio:

4:10   2:15   11:3 (the ratio of 11 to 3)

• Use the colon to distinguish a main title from a subtitle, and a chapter from a verse or section:

The Dragons of Eden: Speculations on the Evolution of Human Intelligence
Exodus 8:3–7 (Chapter 8, verses 3 through 7)
Chapter 2: Section 8

• Use the colon after the salutation in a business letter:

Dear Mr. Koman: Dear Sirs:

• Place colons outside of quotation marks when they are not part of the quoted material:

Only one of his letters refers to the codeword "swordfish": the one dated February 14, 1932.

PERIOD

• Use a period as the final mark of punctuation in a declarative or mildly imperative sentence:

> All Arabian Peninsula countries, except Yemen, produce oil.
>
> Consider your options carefully.

• Use a period as the final mark of punctuation after an indirect quotation:

> Franklin D. Roosevelt was the man who said that the only thing we have to fear is fear itself.

Compare the indirect quotation, above, with a direct quotation:

> Franklin D. Roosevelt said: "The only thing we have to fear is fear itself."

• Use periods with most abbreviations:

apt.	assoc.	atty.	ref.	tbsp.
M.A.	Esq.	Mr.	Mrs.	Ph.D.

• Use one period to conclude a sentence ending with an abbreviation:

> The package should be shipped to Ms. Gail Jones, Pres.

Exception: Periods are frequently omitted in the abbreviations of organizations and national and international agencies:

NBC	NFL	NATO	UNICEF	IBM

Consult a dictionary for the accepted punctuation of abbreviations.

QUESTION MARK

• Use a question mark after a direct question:

> Who were the first four presidents of the United States?

• Use a question mark after a direct question within a declarative sentence. Notice that no comma is needed after a question mark to separate a quotation from the remainder of a sentence.

"Why do my ears itch?" the patient asked.

"Who believes in ghosts?" the woman said, attempting to calm her husband.

When a question mark concludes a quotation at the end of a sentence, no period is needed.

The patient asked, "Why do my ears itch?"

The woman attempted to calm her husband by saying, "Who believes in ghosts?"

• Use a question mark or a period as the final punctuation for a request:

Would you please send me a copy of all of our correspondence with the National Instrument Company?

OR

Would you please send me a copy of all of our correspondence with the National Instrument Company.

• Use question marks when each item of the series poses a separate question:

Under what circumstances will you be receiving shipment? paying for freight? paying for insurance?

Note: When the sense of a question is not completed until the final word of a series, use only one question mark:

Is Kate right-handed, left-handed, or ambidextrous?

• Use a question mark when the final clause of a compound sentence is a question:

Here is the crucial issue: will the plane be ready for testing by the first of May?

We may be able to meet the deadline, but are you willing to risk skipping final safety checks for the sake of a schedule?

- Use a question mark enclosed by parentheses to indicate doubt about some item of information:

    Jane Seymour, the third wife of Henry VIII, was born in 1510(?) and died in 1537.

EXCLAMATION POINT

- Use the exclamation point after emphatic statements, commands, and interjections:

    I must have those documents!
    Leave this room immediately!
    Never! Hand them over!

- Use an exclamation point after an exclamatory interjection or statement quoted within a declarative sentence. Notice that no comma is needed after an exclamation point to separate a quotation from the remainder of a sentence.

    "Incredible!" he said.
    "I don't believe my own eyes!" she gasped.

When an exclamation point concludes a quotation at the end of a sentence, no period is needed.

    Mimi ran to the foot of the stairs and yelled: "The astronauts have landed on Mars!"

QUOTATION MARKS

Quotation marks occur in pairs and indicate the beginning and end of material quoted from a written or spoken source.

- Use quotation marks to enclose direct quotations. The first word of the quoted material is capitalized:

"The plants need watering," he said.
Gladys answered, "So what are you waiting for?"

When quotations are interrupted by nonquoted material, the first word of the second part of the quotation is capitalized only if it begins a new sentence:

"My work is my passion," wrote De Silva in a letter to his wife, "now that you are so many miles away."

"Visit soon," he added. "When we're apart, a madness overcomes me."

• Use single quotation marks to indicate a quotation within a quotation:

Mr. Thule promptly answered the request and wrote, "We are enclosing our pamphlet, 'How to Learn Electronics in your Home,' for a nominal fee."

In her letter, Ms. Ryan added: "I am enclosing the lyrics to my latest song, 'Country Blue.' "

• Use quotation marks to enclose the titles of short works: short stories, essays, short poems, songs, chapters from a book, articles or sections from magazines or newspapers, etc. (Titles of long works—books, magazines, newspapers, albums, long poems, etc. —are underlined when typewritten and italicized when typeset.)

"How Tom Brangwen Married a Polish Lady" is the title of the first chapter of D. H. Lawrence's *The Rainbow*.

On receiving *The Washington Post* in the morning, I read the front page, the comics, and then the "Style" section.

• Use quotation marks to indicate words that receive special emphasis. (Some writers prefer italics for this purpose.)

"Game" is a difficult word to define when one considers that the term includes basketball, chess, and military exercises.
OR
Game is a difficult word to define.

Note: Avoid overusing quotation marks to emphasize technical terms, humorous or trite expressions, or common nicknames:

OVERUSED: "Big Bob" Hanson could "eat a bear" for lunch.

IMPROVED: Bob Hanson had an enormous appetite.

Punctuating Quotations

• Introduce a quotation with a comma or a colon. (Lengthy and/or formal quotations are introduced by colons.) Place commas and periods inside final quotation marks:

"The plants need watering," he repeated.

She turned to him: "It wouldn't give you a hernia to lift the watering can once a year."

The President announced: "I emphatically support equal rights for women, but I oppose the Equal Rights Amendment."

Note: If a parenthetical reference follows a quotation and ends a sentence, the period should be placed after the closing parenthesis:

Swanson writes that she "believes in invisible forces" (p. 211).

• Place a semicolon or a colon outside of quoted material unless it is part of the quoted passage:

Mark Stilson swore that he consumed "no less than three hundred marshmallows at one sitting"; however, there were no witnesses and the judges required him to repeat his achievement.

Two things happened after I read Poe's "The Raven": I developed a fear of large black birds and insisted that I be asleep by the first stroke of midnight.

• Place a question mark, exclamation point, or dash inside the final quotation mark if it applies to the quoted material; place it outside if it applies to the entire sentence:

QUESTION MARKS

The officer asked, "Do you usually drive on the shoulder of the road?"

Was Israel Putnam the one who said, "Don't fire till you see the whites of their eyes"?

EXCLAMATION MARKS

The child screamed: "I won't!"

Don't you dare use that tone of voice to say, "Thank you"!

DASHES

What Mr. Larder thought to be his pithiest advice—"He who keeps an open mouth will one day find a pigeon roosting there" —confused more people than it enlightened.

"How could a good kid like you—" Thomas turned away, unwilling to finish the accusation.

• When quoting dialogue, begin a new paragraph with every change of speaker:

"It's the Russian princess, don't you know?" I answered; "the one with the 'golden eyes,' in black velvet."

"Golden eyes? I *say!*" cried Miss Churm, while my companions watched her with intensity as she withdrew.   HENRY JAMES

• When a direct quotation, in dialogue, extends for two or more paragraphs, place quotation marks at the beginning of each paragraph and at the end of the final paragraph:

Phillips continued: "I was not aware that a person could be so easily offended. And in any event, I only told the truth.

"However, if an apology is called for, I'll be happy to oblige— as long as I don't have to retract my views. If I have offended you by speaking my mind, then I'm sorry. The fact that I think your generosity is motivated by guilt reflects badly on me, I'm sure. At all costs, develop a thicker skin. Not everyone is going to love you."

- In essays and business correspondence, quotations of three or more lines are indented five spaces and set off from the body of the text. No quotation marks are used when a passage is indented in this way.

> In *Anna Karenina,* Tolstoy draws a striking analogy between the character Levin and a tree in springtime:
>
> > Spring is the time for making plans and resolutions, and Levin, like a tree which in the spring-time does not yet know in which direction and in what manner its young shoots and twigs (still imprisoned in their buds) will develop, did not quite know what work on his beloved land he was going to take in hand, but he felt that his mind was full of the finest plans and resolutions.

ELLIPSIS

- Use the ellipsis mark (three spaced periods) to indicate that you've omitted words within quoted material:

> While animals use only a few limited cries . . . human beings use extremely complicated systems of sputtering, hissing, gurgling, clucking, cooing noises called *language.*   S. I. HAYAKAWA

Note: When the omitted material indicated by an ellipsis mark ends a sentence, a fourth period is added:

> Oranges do not bruise one another the way apples sometimes do, and an orange, in fact, can absorb a blow that would finish an apple. . . .   JOHN MCPHEE

- Use an ellipsis mark to indicate a pause or uncompleted statement in dialogue:

> "Diana, would you please . . . Never mind, I'll do it myself."

BRACKETS

- Use brackets to separate your own remarks from the material you are quoting:

"I made Cumberland [a town of 40,000 in western Maryland] my home," said Ms. Hopkins, "because it is situated in the mountains but is only four hours from the sea."

• When quoting material that contains an error in spelling or word choice, enclose the Latin word *sic* (meaning *thus* or *exactly as shown*) in brackets to indicate that the error has been made by the quoted author, not by you:

> The chairman of the board has written: "The introduction of computers into the home will have a tremendous affect [*sic*] on the American economy."

• Use brackets to set off a parenthetical remark within a parenthetical remark:

> Ms. Hopkins said that she made Cumberland (a town in western Maryland [pop. 40,000]) her home because it was situated in the mountains but was only four hours from the sea.

APOSTROPHE

• An apostrophe (and the letter *s*, in most cases) is used to indicate possession:

> the cat's fur (the fur of the cat)
> the man's mistake (the mistake made by the man)

• Depending on the spelling of a noun, use one of the following variants of the apostrophe and the letter *s* to show possession:

To a singular noun not ending in *s*, add an apostrophe and *s*:

> Bob's ice cream   the book's cover
> the girl's new dress

To a singular noun ending in *s*, add an apostrophe and *s* if the resulting word is not difficult to pronounce; otherwise, add only an apostrophe. (One consideration in determining the ease of pronunciation is the first letter of the word following the possessive form. When the first letter has an *s* or *z* sound, only an apostrophe is used.)

the waitress's uniform	the waitress' secret
James's basketball	James' zest for living
the dress's material	the dress' size

To a plural noun not ending in *s*, add an apostrophe and *s:*

women's league   men's ties   children's department

To a plural noun ending in *s*, add only an apostrophe:

carpenters' union   eighty cents' worth   boys' camp

To personal pronouns, do not add an apostrophe. Use the possessive case of the personal pronoun:

his	hers	ours
theirs	yours	its

To indefinite pronouns, add an apostrophe and *s:*

one's devotion   someone's basket   everybody's business

To compound nouns or word groups functioning as nouns, add an apostrophe and *s* to the final word:

brother-in-law's apartment	the Foreign Minister's plane
the Rotary Club's bus	the Secretary of State's mission

(By contrast, to make a compound noun plural, add *s* to the first word: brother*s*-in-law, Secretar*ies* of State.)

To indicate *joint* ownership, add an apostrophe and *s* to the *last* person or thing named in a series:

Pete and Betty's bicycle

(The bicycle belongs to both Pete and Betty.)

To indicate *individual* ownership, add an apostrophe and *s* to *each* person or thing named in a series:

Pete's and Betty's bicycles

(There are two bicycles: one belongs to Pete; the other, to Betty.)

● Use an apostrophe to indicate an omission of letters in a contraction:

don't (do not)   we'll (we will)   haven't (have not)

Note: Do not confuse contractions with the possessive case pronouns *its*, *their*, and *whose:*

"it's"   (a contraction that means "it is")
"they're"   (a contraction that means "they are")
"who's"   (a contraction that means "who is")

● The identity of numerals replaced by an apostrophe is established by the context of a passage. If you are referring to an event in your own life and write "the summer of '73," it is understood that you mean 1973. If you are reporting on the American Civil War and write "the winter of '63," it is understood that you mean 1863.

● Use an apostrophe and an *s* to form the plural of letters, words referred to as words, and numbers. The letter, word, or number being made plural should be underlined when typed or handwritten and italicized when typeset. The apostrophe and *s* should not be italicized.

Her *o*'s cannot be distinguished from her *e*'s.

His *occasion*'s are misspelled throughout the paragraph.

Ten *2*'s make twenty.

Note: When forming the plural of a proper noun, omit the apostrophe before the *s*.

There are three *Albert*s working at our office.

● Use an apostrophe and an *s* to form the plural of symbols, years in decades, and abbreviations that include periods. Do not italicize the year, abbreviation, or symbol that has been made plural.

The frequent ***'s throughout the notice are distracting.

The 1980's do not seem as politically volatile as the 1960's.

Many people who have Ph.D.'s are driving cabs for a living.

Note: The apostrophe may be omitted in forming the plural of a decade, of an abbreviation with no periods, or of a symbol:

1980s   CPAs   *s

DASH

Dashes—indicated on a typewriter by two hyphen marks—should be used with care, since they abruptly change the rhythm of a sentence. Overuse of dashes makes a sentence or a paragraph difficult to read.

• Use a dash to mark a sudden change in thought or tone:

He said, "I'd like you to go and—Never mind. I'll do it myself."

• Use a dash for emphasis and clarity in setting off introductory remarks:

From Bangor to Baltimore—east coast gamblers have forsaken Las Vegas for the charms of Atlantic City.

• Use a dash for emphasis and clarity in setting off a repeated structure, an appositive phrase, or a parenthetical remark (especially when these are presented in a series):

A REPEATED STRUCTURE

The advances of the age are advances in mechanism—in radio and television, in electronics, in jet planes. A. S. NEILL

AN APPOSITIVE PHRASE

Altitude sickness—an illness that strikes those not used to mountain elevations—frequently disrupts the plans of tourists.

A PARENTHETICAL REMARK

All the pupils brought their dinners in baskets—corn dodger, buttermilk, and other good things—and sat in the shade of the trees at noon and ate them. MARK TWAIN

PARENTHESES

• Use parentheses to enclose information that is not essential to the meaning of a sentence. The information may define, illustrate, comment on, or otherwise supplement the word or words preceding the parentheses. Commas, dashes, and parentheses are all used to set off parenthetical remarks.

Using dashes is the most emphatic method:

> In order to pass gymnasium—and you had to pass it to graduate—you had to learn to swim if you didn't know how.

Using parentheses is the least emphatic method:

> In order to pass gymnasium (and you had to pass it to graduate) you had to learn to swim if you didn't know how.
> JAMES THURBER

Using commas is a mildly emphatic method:

> In order to pass gymnasium, and you had to pass it to graduate, you had to learn to swim if you didn't know how.

• Though parenthetical material may be deleted from a sentence without disrupting its meaning, the information within parentheses is part of the sentence's grammatical structure. Be certain that a sentence reads smoothly with its parenthetical elements.

AWKWARD   In solving the case of "The Speckled Band," Sherlock Holmes observed several important but obscure details (the dish of milk by the safe).

IMPROVED   In solving the case of "The Speckled Band," Sherlock Holmes observed several important but obscure details (one of which—the dish of milk by the safe—led him to conclude that the speckled band was a deadly snake).

- Use parentheses to set off the numbers or letters that introduce items in a series. (When numbered items are listed, as opposed to being written out in one sentence, the numbers are not enclosed in parentheses.)

> There are good reasons why small colleges have had their troubles lately: (1) the costs of maintenance and faculty salaries are rising; (2) the number of potential applicants has declined with the end of the baby boom; and (3) many people no longer believe that a college degree is *the* key to success.

> There are good reasons why small colleges have had their troubles lately:
> 1. The costs of maintenance and faculty salaries are rising.
> 2. The number of potential applicants has declined with the end of the baby boom.
> 3. Many people no longer believe that a college degree is *the* key to success.

- Punctuate the words within parentheses as you would any other group of words. When parenthetical matter ends a sentence, follow the punctuation below:

> Thomas questions the military's contention that spare parts are being purchased at reasonable prices (p. 401).

> The train pulled into Union Depot (one of the oldest railroad stations in America).

> The train pulled into Union Depot. (It is one of the oldest railroad stations in America.)

Note: When a sentence is enclosed within parentheses (as in this last example), a period is placed within the parentheses.

SLASH

- Use a slash mark to indicate an option:

> Poor water pressure and/or cloudy tap water can indicate clogged pipes inside a house or a broken main outside.

• Use a slash mark to indicate the end of a line of poetry when two or more lines have been run together in quoted material:

It was T. S. Eliot who wrote: "We only live, only suspire/Consumed by either fire or fire."

11

The Mechanics of Writing

The term *mechanics,* applied to writing, refers to the rules regarding capitalization, underlining, abbreviation, hyphenation, word division, and the presentation of numbers. These rules are conventional: that is, they have been agreed upon over time and are so taken for granted that writers exercise virtually no judgment in applying them. Because of the wide agreement regarding, for instance, the conditions under which a noun should be capitalized, failure to adhere to the rules of capitalization—or any other rule of mechanics—will distract your reader and thus interfere with the process of communication.

CAPITALIZATION

The rules that follow summarize the uses of capitalization in most general writing and correspondence. When in doubt as to whether a word should be capitalized, consult a recent unabridged dictionary.

• Capitalize the first word of a sentence.

He is more powerful than a speeding locomotive.
Who is that man?

Exception: When questions are presented as phrases in a series, each item of which poses a new question, capitalization of each phrase is optional. Both sentences below are correctly capitalized:

> Who is that man? the woman to his left? the older man behind them?
> Who is that man? The woman to his left? The older man behind them?

• For titles of books, plays, magazines, periodicals, and works of art, capitalize the first and last words and all remaining words *except* prepositions, articles, and conjunctions fewer than five letters in length. If the word *the* is not part of a title, it is not capitalized:

> *For Whom the Bell Tolls*   *King Lear*
> "A Rose for Emily"   *The Economist*
> *The Boston Globe*   the *Mona Lisa*
> *The Thinker*   the *TV Guide*

• Capitalize the word in a title that immediately follows a colon or a semicolon:

> *The Uses of Enchantment: The Meaning and Importance of Fairy Tales*

• Capitalize proper nouns, including the names of racial and ethnic groups; countries, their citizens, and their languages; religions and the adherents of a religion; political parties; and schools of art:

> Spain   Buddhism   Mrs. Keating
> Spaniard   Buddhist   the Democrats
> Spanish   Oriental   Romanticism
> China   Chinese   Gothic

Exceptions: Do not capitalize *black* or *white* when referring to racial groups.

• Capitalize proper adjectives (adjectives derived from proper nouns):

> *American*-style pizza   a *Machiavellian* mind
> an *English* sense of humor

Exceptions: *Oriental* is usually capitalized, though it appears occasionally with a lower-case *o:* an oriental rug. *Biblical* and *biblical* are both considered correct.

• Capitalize the names of specific geographical places, regions, and political divisions, including the names of cities, towns, counties, streets, parks, mountains, valleys, etc.:

Illinois	Mount Rushmore	the South
Cook County	Napa Valley	the East Coast
Chicago	Elm Street	the Northwest
Precinct Five	Arlington Heights	the West

Note: Common nouns such as *elm, five,* and *heights* are capitalized when used in proper names. (See also page 151.)

• Capitalize the names of the days of the week, months, and holidays:

Monday   October   Columbus Day

Note: Centuries and decades should be written out in lower-case letters:

the twenty-first century   the fifties (or the '50s)

• Capitalize the names of governmental assemblies, departments, and bureaus:

the United States Congress
the Department of the Interior
the Federal Bureau of Investigation

Note: Prepositions, articles, and conjunctions in titles of government assemblies and agencies are not capitalized unless they are longer than five letters.

• Capitalize the names of athletic, philanthropic, and social clubs or organizations:

the New York Mets
the Knights of Columbus
Physicians for Social Responsibility

• Capitalize titles of rank when they *precede* a name; do not capitalize them if they follow a name or are not associated with a specific name:

Governor Smith   Mr. Allen Smith, governor of Florida
Mayor Koch   Mr. Edward Koch, mayor of New York City

Exceptions: Titles of high rank may be capitalized without being paired with a proper name.

The President arrived in California on Friday.

• Capitalize titles and the abbreviations of titles that follow a name in an address:

Frank Sladko, Esq.
Max Perkins, Editor

• Capitalize the names attributed to God by various religious groups; also capitalize the names of sacred literature:

Allah   Lord   Buddha
Jehovah   King of Kings   Yahweh
the Bible   the Upanishads   the Koran

Note: The pronouns *he, his,* and *him* should be capitalized when referring to the Supreme Being:

The man prayed to God in the hope that He might guide him.

• Capitalize the names of particular ships, automobiles, monuments, dams, buildings, etc.

the USS *Eisenhower*   the Lincoln Memorial
the Volkswagen Rabbit   Liberty Dam

• Capitalize the names of historical events, periods, and documents:

the American Civil War
the Bronze Age
the Declaration of Independence

• Capitalize the pronoun *I* and the interjection *O.* The word *oh* is capitalized only when it begins a sentence:

> O wild West Wind, thou breath of Autumn's being,
>
> . . .
>
> Wild Spirit, which art moving everywhere;
> Destroyer and preserver; hear, oh hear!
>
> . . .
>
> Oh! lift me as a wave, a leaf, a cloud!
> I fall upon the thorns of life! I bleed!
>
> PERCY BYSSHE SHELLEY

• Capitalize brand-name products:

> Breck® shampoo
> Crest® toothpaste

• Capitalize compound words as follows:

The prefix *ex* is not capitalized unless it begins a sentence:

> Please welcome ex-Chairman Grose.

Capitalize the first word of a compound used as part of a proper noun:

> Fifty-third Street
> the Sixty-second World Series

• Capitalize all words in titles of distinction:

> The Right Reverend _____
> Vice President _____
> First Lieutenant _____

• Capitalize abbreviations formed from capitalized words. Also capitalize the short forms of specific proper names:

> UN   NATO   U.S.A.   IBM   AFL-CIO
> the Channel (English Channel)   the Continent (of Europe)

• **Do not capitalize** the name of a season, unless it is personified:

spring   Spring's maidenhood
summer   Summer's passion
fall/autumn   Autumn's bluster
winter   Winter's roar

• **Do not capitalize** *north, south, east, west,* or any combination of these—unless the direction is used as a noun and refers to a particular area of a country:

We will be traveling northwest for most of the trip.

(The direction is used as an adverb.)

We will be spending some time in the Northwest before arriving in Alaska.

(The direction is used as a noun, the object of a preposition.)

• **Do not capitalize** *uncle, aunt, father, mother,* etc.—unless they are used as proper names or as parts of proper names:

my aunt   my father   my mother
Aunt Freda   Uncle Isaac   "Come here, Father!"

ITALICS/UNDERLINING

Underlining a handwritten or typewritten word is the equivalent of typesetting that word in italics. The rules that follow summarize the uses of underlining in most general writing and correspondence.

• Underline the titles of books, plays, works of art, magazines, periodicals, movies, and shows on television and radio. (Note: the word *the* is underlined only when it is part of a title.)

King Lear   The Great Gatsby   Hill Street Blues
High Noon   the Mona Lisa   The Shadow

Exception: The titles of religious and legal documents are not underlined:

the Koran   the Bible   the Voting Rights Act
the Constitution   the Upanishads

• Underline words that are being defined in a sentence:

Ceres was the Roman goddess of agriculture.

Note: Words being defined may be placed in quotation marks:

"Ceres" was the Roman goddess of agriculture.

• Underline words receiving special emphasis or words referred to as words:

Are you going to that game?
Are you going to that game?
The word zoo has an interesting history.

Note: Do not overuse underlining (i.e., italics) for emphasis. If most of the words in a sentence are underlined, the emphasis on any one word is diminished.

• Underline letters and numbers made plural with an apostrophe and an s. (See page 141 for a related discussion.)

A Scrabble® board has only four o's and far too many i's.
Double 6's in backgammon is usually a good roll.

• Underline the names of trains, ships, aircraft, and spacecraft:

the Washingtonian (a train)   the Albatross (an airplane)
the USS Eisenhower (a ship)   Voyager 1 (a spacecraft)

• Underline foreign words that have not yet been incorporated into English:

blanc   amore
chéri   coup de grâce
chutzpah   vino

Foreign words that *have* been incorporated into English are not underlined:

malaise	chalet
hors d'oeuvre	nuance
falsetto	prima donna

ABBREVIATIONS

In business correspondence and academic writing, use abbreviations sparingly.

● Use abbreviations for titles of rank both before and after a proper name:

Dr. Wilson	Mary Wilson, M.D.
St. Jerome	Bruce Jones, B.A.
Mr. Roosevelt	Alan Fox, C.P.A.
Mrs. Clay	Fred Walsh, Jr.
Ms. Fairbanks	

(Actually *Ms.* is not an abbreviation, though it is often followed by a period. Both *Ms.* and *Ms* are acceptable.)

Note: The words "doctor" and "saint" should *not* be abbreviated when they do not precede a proper name:

When are you going to see the doctor?
Mr. Henderson is a saint.

● Use the following abbreviations with dates and numbers:

A.D. 1600 *(anno domini)*, "in the year of the Lord"

500 B.C. (before Christ)

2:01 P.M. or 2:01 p.m. *(post meridiem, "after noon")*

2:01 A.M. or 2:01 a.m. *(ante meridiem, "before noon")*

No. 6 or no. 6 (number 6)

$12.40 (twelve dollars and forty cents)

• Use accepted abbreviations of the District of Columbia (D.C.); the United States of America (U.S.A. or USA, U.S. or US); the Union of Soviet Socialist Republics (U.S.S.R. or USSR); common acronyms—abbreviations that form pronounceable words (NATO, NASA); accepted abbreviations of names (JFK, FDR); accepted abbreviations of organizations, agencies, and companies (USDA, CBS, UN, IBM); and accepted abbreviations of polysyllabic scientific terms (DNA—deoxyribonucleic acid; TNT—trinitrotoluene).

• Know the meanings of Latin abbreviations before using them. (English translations of these abbreviations are frequently spelled out.)

cf. *(confer)*	compare
e.g. *(exempli gratia)*	for example
et al. *(et alii)*	and others
etc. *(et cetera)*	and so forth
i.e. *(id est)*	that is
v., vs. *(versus)*	against
viz. *(videlicet)*	namely

Note: When the abbreviation *i.e.*, *e.g.*, or *viz.* begins a parenthetical remark, it is followed by a comma, as it would be if translated into English:

There are good reasons why private colleges have been in financial trouble (viz., applications are down, costs are up, and the perception that college is the one key to success has all but disappeared).
      OR
There are good reasons why private colleges have been in trouble (namely, applications are down . . .).

• Do not abbreviate the following words unless you are copying an abbreviation that appears in a corporate name or in the title of an organization:

Avenue, Street, Boulevard, or any geographical designation (such as Mountain):

NOT	1251 Seton Ave.
BUT	1251 Seton Avenue

Company, Incorporated, or Limited:

NOT   National Instrument Co.
BUT   National Instrument Company

The names of countries, states, or cities. (Exceptions: U.S.A. and U.S.S.R. are standard abbreviations.)

NOT   N.Y., N.Y.
BUT   New York, New York

A first name or the name of a month or day:

NOT   Wm. Courtney was born on Fri., Aug. 12, 1983.
BUT   William Courtney was born on Friday, August 12, 1983.

The names of courses of instruction and measurements:

NOT   In marine bio. we saw a lobster that weighed 22 lbs.
BUT   In marine biology we saw a lobster that weighed twenty-
       two pounds.

The words *volume, chapter,* and *page:*

NOT   Turn to Vol. 1, Chap. 2, p. 793.
BUT   Turn to Volume 1, Chapter 2, page 793.

HYPHENATION

• Use a hyphen to join compound adjectives, two or more words functioning as a single adjective.

   a good-luck charm
   an emerald-green suit

Exceptions: If the same words forming the compound are placed *after* a noun, a hyphen should not be used:

   She kept the charm for good luck.
   The suit was emerald green.

Do not place a hyphen after an adverb ending in *-ly:*

   extraordinarily good luck
   a happily ended affair

• Use hyphens in a series of compound adjectives when the noun being modified appears only once:

> Did you get a first-, second-, or third-place prize?

• Place a hyphen after the prefixes *ex-* and *self-* and before the suffix *-elect*:

> ex-convict
> self-expression
> senator-elect

Place a hyphen after the prefixes *pro-*, *anti-*, and *pre-* only when they are joined to words beginning with a capital letter:

> pro-French   pre-Wilson   profascist
> anti-German   predetermined   antisocial

When the prefixes *de-*, *pre-*, and *re-* are positioned before words beginning with the letter *e*, use a hyphen to prevent mispronunciation:

> de-escalate   pre-exist   re-examine
> de-emphasize   pre-establish   re-educate

Place a hyphen between the prefix *co-* and a root word according to current usage. (Consult a dictionary when in doubt.)

> co-ed   coexist
> co-opt   coordinate

Place a hyphen between a single letter used as a prefix and a root word:

> X-rated

• Use hyphens when writing out fractions and numbers from twenty-one to ninety-nine:

> three-eighths   two-thirds
> twenty-five   seventy-three

• Use a hyphen to prevent the misreading of compound words:

> Mr. Pevsner ordered a new service contract.

The meaning of this sentence is unclear. Mr. Pevsner may have ordered a service contract for a recently installed oil burner, in which case the contract would be for new service, or a *new-service contract.* Or he may have been dissatisfied with service on an existing oil burner and arranged a service contract with another company, in which case he'd be ordering a *new service-contract.* The ambiguous sentence can be revised in two ways:

> Mr. Pevsner ordered a new-service contract.
> Mr. Pevsner ordered a new service-contract.

WORD DIVISION

In business correspondence and in academic writing, avoid dividing words (especially proper names) at the end of a line; but when a word division is unavoidable, follow these conventions:

• Divide words at syllable breaks, indicated in most dictionaries by a dot (·):

> may·on·naise
> re·as·sure

• Do not divide a word so that one letter is left at the end of a line or two letters at the beginning of a line:

NOT	Many people are disturbed by the theory that man e-volved from the apes.
BUT	Many people are disturbed by the theory that man evolved from the apes.
NOT	After years of military supremacy, Napoleon was defeat-ed at Waterloo.
BUT	After years of military supremacy, Napoleon was de-feated at Waterloo.

- Hyphenated words should be divided only at the hyphen:

NOT   Because she was interested in preserving her much-admired gardens, Myra Bellington willed her home to the Newport Historical Society.

BUT   Because she was interested in preserving her much-admired gardens, Myra Bellington willed her home to the Newport Historical Society.

- Avoid misleading word divisions:

NOT   As a former campaign manager, Mr. Rollins was indignant at not having been notified of Harriman's press conference.

BUT   As a former campaign manager, Mr. Rollins was indignant at not having been notified of Harriman's press conference.

NUMBERS

Follow these conventions when writing out numbers:

- Write out fractions and numbers that can be expressed in one or two words. Write out the numbers from one to ninety-nine, including ages. Remember to hyphenate the numbers from twenty-one to ninety-nine.

five-eighths	twenty-one
two thousand	five hundred
thirty-one thousand	four million
seventy-one percent	

- Use figures to express phone numbers, rates of speed, street names, page numbers, and military units:

536	1,633,299
2,540	48th Street
651-2121	50 mph
the 52nd Airborne Division	pages 15–18

• Write out a number that begins a sentence:

Five hundred thirty-two clubs participated in the exhibition.
OR
There were 532 clubs participating in the exhibition.

• Large round numbers are expressed as follows:

$2,500,000	two and a half million dollars	$2.5 million
2,250,000	two and a quarter million	2.25 million

• Sums of less than a dollar are expressed in two ways:

$.95   95¢

• Numbers used in dates are expressed as follows:

Conventional style:	August 12, 1957
European (and military) style:	12 August 1957
Embellished style (used for invitations):	August twelfth (when not followed by a year) the twelfth of August (when not followed by a year)
	500 B.C.
	A.D. 649
	from 1775 to 1776
	1775–1776
	1775–76

• Numbers designating time of day are written as follows:

1 P.M. or 1 p.m.
2:30 A.M. or 2:30 a.m.
three o'clock in the afternoon
twenty minutes past six in the evening

• Neither decades nor centuries are capitalized when written out:

the seventies		the '70s
the fourteenth century	OR	the 14th century

PART FOUR

Effective Writing

12

Eliminating Grammatical Errors

Writing is a medium for the exchange of ideas and information. When all is working well—when sentences are grammatical, when words are carefully chosen, when paragraphs are soundly structured—communication is usually successful. Someone or some people read your sentences, understand your meaning, and respond accordingly. But when a piece of writing is flawed, the process of communication breaks down; the transfer of information stops as the reader tries to decipher your meaning.

There are many flaws that can sabotage your writing; among the most serious are ungrammatical sentences. In this chapter, you will learn how to avoid the most common grammatical errors: fragments, run-ons, and comma splices. You will also learn to correct misplaced and dangling modifiers; shifts in person, number, tense, voice, and mood; and faulty pronoun references.

FRAGMENTS

A sentence is an independent clause, which contains a subject and a predicate. It depends on no other group of words for its meaning. A common grammatical error occurs when a fragment—which is a dependent clause or, alternately, a word group that lacks a subject or predicate—is used in place of a complete sentence.

FRAGMENT   in order to secure a good job

SENTENCE   Mrs. Allen believed her daughter should attend college in order to secure a good job.

The above fragment, an infinitive phrase, can be combined with an independent clause to complete its meaning. The infinitive phrase now functions as an adverb, modifying the verb *should attend.*

FRAGMENT   in the basement and in the attic

SENTENCE   We searched for the missing book in the basement and in the attic.

The above fragment, a prepositional phrase, can be combined with an independent clause to complete its meaning. The prepositional phrase now functions as an adverb, modifying the verb *searched.*

FRAGMENT   because oil prices have increased

SENTENCE   Because oil prices have increased, auto manufacturers have designed fuel-efficient cars.

The above fragment is a dependent clause: it has both a subject ("oil prices") and a predicate verb ("have increased"); but since it is preceded by the subordinate conjunction "because," it must be joined to an independent clause to complete its meaning.

Acceptable Uses of Fragments

Fragments may be used in writing to re-create the rhythms of speech:

"You arrived in time, I suppose?"
"Naturally."

In essay or letter writing, the use of fragments is limited— usually to an occasional transition:

There are several good reasons for your joining our firm. **Now for an excellent one.** We are a young company that's ambitious and looking to expand. You have skills that can help us.

RUN-ON SENTENCES

A run-on sentence occurs if two or more independent clauses are joined without a conjunction or appropriate punctuation. *There are five ways to correct a run-on sentence:*

- Identify the two or more sentences that have been run together and separate them with a period.

RUN-ON	Organize a résumé according to your education, work experience, career objectives, and recreational interests review your needs carefully before stating a career objective.
CORRECT	Organize a résumé according to your education, work experience, career objectives, and recreational interests. Review your needs carefully before stating a career objective.

- Use a coordinate conjunction and a comma to join the independent clauses of the run-on sentence. (See pages 13–14 regarding coordinate conjunctions.)

RUN-ON	Employers review the information presented in a résumé they also review how that information is presented.
CORRECT	Employers review the information presented in a résumé, *but* they also review how that information is presented.

If one of the independent clauses in the above run-on sentence contained a comma, then a semicolon (rather than a comma) would be used before the coordinate conjunction.

Employers review the information presented in a résumé; *but* they also review how that information is presented, for the appearance of a document suggests something about its author.

- Use a semicolon to separate the two independent clauses of a run-on sentence—but only if the semicolon is understood to take the place of a comma and a coordinate conjunction.

RUN-ON   A good résumé will include carefully chosen
                    details it will create an impression of depth
                    without inundating the reader with your life
                    history.

CORRECT   A good résumé will include carefully chosen
                    details, *and* it will create an impression of
                    depth without inundating the reader with your
                    life history.

CORRECT   A good résumé will include carefully chosen
                    details; it will create an impression of depth
                    without inundating the reader with your life
                    history.

• Use a semicolon, followed by an adverbial conjunction and a
  comma, to separate the independent clauses of a run-on sentence.
  (See page 15 regarding adverbial conjunctions.)

RUN-ON   A résumé and a cover letter are the first things
                    a potential employer sees associated with your
                    name make sure that both are typed neatly.

CORRECT   A résumé and a cover letter are the first things
                    a potential employer sees associated with your
                    name; *therefore,* make sure that both are typed
                    neatly.

• Use a subordinate conjunction to make one of the clauses of the
  run-on dependent upon the other. If the dependent clause introduces the new sentence, place a comma after it. If the dependent clause ends the sentence, the comma is optional. (See pages
  14–15 regarding subordinate conjunctions.)

> *Since* a résumé and a cover letter are the first things a potential
> employer sees associated with your name, make sure that both are
> typed neatly.

COMMA SPLICES

A comma splice occurs when a writer joins two independent
clauses by using a comma:

Wood stoves are an efficient source of heat, environmentalists are concerned that woodsmoke adds pollutants to the air.

The comma splice is actually an encouraging sign, for the writer has recognized and attempted to show that a sentence contains two independent clauses. The effort, however, is only partially complete, for the result is still ungrammatical. *To eliminate a comma splice, use one of the five methods suggested for eliminating run-on sentences:*

• Separate the independent clauses into two sentences:

 Wood stoves are an efficient source of heat. Environmentalists are concerned that woodsmoke adds pollutants to the air.

• Use a coordinate conjunction and a comma to join the independent clauses:

 Wood stoves are an efficient source of heat, *but* environmentalists are concerned that woodsmoke adds pollutants to the air.

• Use a semicolon to join the independent clauses (if the semicolon is understood to take the place of a comma and a coordinate conjunction):

 Wood stoves are an efficient source of heat; environmentalists are concerned that woodsmoke adds pollutants to the air.

• Use an adverbial conjunction to join the independent clauses:

 Wood stoves are an efficient source of heat; *however,* environmentalists are concerned that woodsmoke adds pollutants to the air.

• Use a subordinate conjunction to make one of the independent clauses grammatically dependent upon the other.

 Although wood stoves are an efficient source of heat, environmentalists are concerned that woodsmoke adds pollutants to the air.

DANGLING MODIFIERS

Modifiers are single words or word groups that qualify the meaning of other words. As such, they are used properly when (1) there is a *definite* word that they modify and (2) they are situated as close to that word as possible.

A modifier is said to "dangle" when the word it modifies has been omitted from a sentence. *To correct this problem, rewrite the sentence to include the modified word:*

INCORRECT	Running up the stairs, the coins fell out of his pocket.
CORRECT	Running up the stairs, *the man* felt the coins falling out of his pocket.
INCORRECT	Enjoying a nap, a bench was the place to stretch out.
CORRECT	*The salesman,* enjoying a nap, was stretched out on a bench.
CORRECT	Enjoying a nap, *the salesman* was stretched out on a bench.

In the sentences labeled "Incorrect," the opening phrases appear to modify the words that immediately follow, which is inaccurate. Benches don't nap, and coins don't run. In the sentences labeled "Correct," the words being modified have been included (and italicized) in the main clause.

MISPLACED MODIFIERS

A modifier is misplaced when it does not clearly refer to the word it modifies.

Misplaced Single-word Modifiers:

Place a single-word modifier next to the word it modifies. The words *only, nearly, hardly, even, almost,* and *just* should be used with care. Changing their location in a sentence results in a change of meaning:

I wanted *only* you to be happy.	*(Only* modifies *you.)*
Only I wanted you to be happy.	*(Only* modifies *I.)*
I *only* wanted you to be happy.	*(Only* modifies *wanted.)*

In everyday conversation, people tend to place a one-word modifier before a verb, even though it may modify another part of the sentence. In your writing, place these modifiers directly before the words they modify.

Misplaced Phrases:

Place a modifying phrase next to the word it modifies:

INCORRECT	Studio musicians work long hours and earn high salaries *in demand.* (The high salaries are not *in demand.)*
CORRECT	Studio musicians *in demand* work long hours and earn high salaries. (The prepositional phrase functions as an adjective modifying "musicians.")
INCORRECT	The attendant took the coats and gave them to the customers *from the closet.* (The customers are not *from the closet.)*
CORRECT	The attendant took the coats *from the closet* and gave them to the customers. (The prepositional phrase functions as an adverb modifying "took." The phrase is not placed directly next to "took" because a verb and its direct object should not be split by a modifier. See the following general rule.)

Misplaced Clauses:

Place a dependent clause next to the word it modifies, unless this disrupts the meaning of the sentence:

INCORRECT	The nurse quickly aided the patient *who was on call.*
	(The nurse, not the patient, was on call.)
CORRECT	The nurse *who was on call* quickly aided the patient.
INCORRECT	The building had once been the site of a grocery *that is for sale.*
	(The building, not the grocery, is for sale.)
CORRECT	The building *that is for sale* had once been the site of a grocery.

A modifier is misplaced when it disrupts the meaning of a sentence by separating subjects from predicates; verbs or infinitives from their objects; or verbs from their auxiliaries.

• *Do not split a subject and its predicate with lengthy modifiers.*

INCORRECT	The foreman, *by offering a generous incentive plan,* encouraged his workers to improve their production.
CORRECT	*By offering a generous incentive plan,* the foreman encouraged his workers to improve their production.
INCORRECT	The man *whom I would recommend because of his imaginative approach to problems, his ability to work well with subordinates, and his extensive experience in the field* is Gerald Watkins.
CORRECT	I would recommend Gerald Watkins *because of his imaginative approach to problems, his ability to work well with subordinates, and his extensive experience in the field.*

• *Do not split a verb and its object with either brief or lengthy modifiers.*

INCORRECT	The press corps did not believe that the crime justified *in any way* the verdict.
CORRECT	The press corps did not believe that the crime *in any way* justified the verdict.

• *Do not split an auxiliary verb and a main verb with lengthy modifiers.*

INCORRECT	The defendant had, *with all the publicity surrounding the trial,* believed that if convicted he would receive a suspended sentence.
CORRECT	*With all the publicity surrounding the trial,* the defendant had believed that if convicted he would receive a suspended sentence.

• *Do not split an infinitive with a lengthy modifier.*

INCORRECT	He hoped to *in the months following the trial* write a book.
CORRECT	He hoped to write a book *in the months following the trial.*

(See second note on page 42 for a discussion of when split infinitives are acceptable.)

A modifier is misplaced when it can be read to modify the words on either side of it. To eliminate a *squinting modifier,* rewrite the sentence so that the modifier refers to one word.

INCORRECT	Going bowling *often* leaves me with a sore arm. (Does *often* modify "bowling" or "leaves"?)
CORRECT	Going bowling can often leave me with a sore arm.
CORRECT	When I bowl often, I get a sore arm.

The way in which you rephrase a sentence with a squinting modifier depends upon your intended meaning.

INCORRECT	The notes that Paul thought he understood *thoroughly* confused him during the interview. (Does *thoroughly* modify "understood" or "confused"?)
CORRECT	The notes, which Paul thought he understood *thoroughly,* confused him during the interview. (*Thoroughly* modifies "understood.")
CORRECT	The notes, which Paul thought he understood, *thoroughly* confused him during the interview. (*Thoroughly* modifies "confused.")

SHIFTS

A *shift,* in the vocabulary of grammar, is an abrupt change of perspective within a sentence (or between sentences). On the following pages are examples showing how to maintain a consistent perspective in your writing.

Shifts in Person

Person is a term describing the identity of the subject of a sentence. The subject can be the person who is speaking (first person), the one who is spoken to (second person), or the one who is spoken about (third person).

	SINGULAR	PLURAL
FIRST PERSON	I	we
SECOND PERSON	you	you
THIRD PERSON	he, she, it, one, a person	they, people

• Avoid shifting from one person to another within a sentence; otherwise, the meaning of the sentence is obscured.

INCORRECT	*People* are tempted to go off their diets when *we* go on vacation. (a shift from third person to first person)
CORRECT	*People* are tempted to go off their diets when *they* go on vacation.
INCORRECT	When *one* engages in this sort of activity, *you* should be prepared for the consequences. (a shift from third person to second)
CORRECT	When *a person* engages in this sort of activity, *he* (or *she*) should be prepared for the consequences.
CORRECT	When *you* engage in this sort of activity, *you* should be prepared for the consequences.

Shifts in Number

Number indicates whether a word is singular or plural. The meaning of a sentence becomes unclear when singular pronouns refer to plural nouns, or plural pronouns refer to singular nouns.

INCORRECT	If the *books* belong to the boy, return *it*. ("Books" is plural; the pronoun "it" is singular.)
CORRECT	If the *book* belongs to the boy, return *it*.
CORRECT	If the *books* belong to the boy, return *them*.

Shifts in Tense

• Avoid shifting tenses within a sentence or a paragraph unless the shift is required by logic. (For a discussion of verb tenses, see Chapter 8.)

INCORRECT	Mrs. Hopkins *arrives* at her desk and *went* directly to work. (a shift from the present tense to the past tense)
IMPROVED	Mrs. Hopkins *arrived* at her desk and *went* directly to work.
IMPROVED	Mrs. Hopkins *arrives* at her desk and *goes* directly to work.

Shifts in Mood

There are three standard moods (sometimes called modes) in English, each of which reveals a specific attitude that the writer or speaker adopts toward his or her subject matter. The mood of a sentence can be determined by examining the main verb. (See pages 108–9 for a detailed discussion of mood.)

The **indicative mood** suggests that the writer believes the subject matter of the sentence to be factual. Most sentences are expressed in the indicative mood:

A whale can weigh as much as ten elephants.

The **subjunctive mood** expresses doubt or a condition contrary to fact. "Would" is a common auxiliary for the subjunctive mood, because it suggests uncertainty about the future. Often, a sentence in the subjunctive mood is introduced by the word *if:*

If I were pleased, I would have said so.

The **imperative mood** expresses a command:

Close the door!

• Avoid shifts of mood within a sentence.

INCORRECT	If he *were* to arrive on the early train, we *will be able* to keep our appointment. (a shift from the subjunctive mood to the indicative)
CORRECT	If he *were* to arrive on the early train, we *would be able* to keep our appointment.
INCORRECT	*Pick up* the pencil in your right hand and you *should hold* it at a forty-five-degree angle to the paper. (a shift from the imperative mood to the subjunctive)
CORRECT	*Pick up* the pencil in your right hand and *hold* it at a forty-five-degree angle to the paper.

Shifts in Voice

Voice is a term that indicates whether the writer has emphasized the *doer* of the action (active voice) or the *receiver* of the action (passive voice). (For a detailed discussion of the active and passive voices, see pages 105–7.)

• Avoid shifting voices within a sentence. The result is usually awkward:

INCORRECT	We *went* to the post office and the letters *were mailed.*
	(The verbs shift from the active voice to the passive.)
CORRECT	We *went* to the post office and *mailed* the letters.

• On occasion, a shift in voices is preferable to no shift.

PREFERABLE	The woman who foiled the robbery attempt *was introduced* and *gave* an impressive speech.
	(The verbs shift from the passive voice to the active.)
LESS PREFERABLE	The mayor *introduced* the woman who foiled the robbery attempt, and she *gave* an impressive speech.
	(Both verbs are expressed in the active voice.)

The first example is preferable to the second because a *single subject*—the woman—remains the focus throughout.

Shifts in Tone

The *tone* of your writing can be formal or informal; jovial or somber; excited or calm; and more. *Tone* refers to qualities of language—word choice, sentence structure—that create for the reader an impression about your work and you, the writer. The tone that you adopt should be geared to a specific audience, for a specific purpose. *Once you adopt a certain tone, use it consis-*

tently. Abrupt shifts will confuse the reader. (For a discussion on choosing the appropriate tone, see pages 230–31.)

INCONSISTENT	In your letter of May 16, 1984, you requested that we pay the balance of our bill—in the amount of $25.31. You know, if you people would get your act together and correct the problems we told you about, maybe you'd get paid.
CONSISTENT	In your letter of May 16, 1984, you requested that we pay the balance of our bill—in the amount of $25.31. Unfortunately, we are not satisfied with the quality of your product. Once you correct the problems we've discussed, you will receive payment.

Shifts in Discourse

Words that are actually spoken by someone—and thus are placed in quotation marks—are referred to as *direct discourse:*

> Mr. Martin crooned to his audience: "Everybody loves somebody sometime."

Words that are attributed to a speaker but that are not actually spoken—and thus are *not* placed in quotation marks— are referred to as *indirect discourse.* Indirect discourse is usually introduced by the word *that* or *whether.*

> Mr. Martin crooned to his audience that everybody loves somebody sometime.

• Avoid shifting within a sentence from direct to indirect discourse (or vice versa).

INCORRECT	The chef wanted to know whether the fish was fresh and "Was the meat tender?" (a shift from indirect to direct discourse)
CORRECT	The chef wanted to know whether the fish was fresh and whether the meat was tender.
CORRECT	The chef asked: "Is the fish fresh? Is the meat tender?"

AMBIGUOUS PRONOUN REFERENCE

Pronoun reference is a term that describes the relationship between a pronoun and its antecedent. An *antecedent* is the noun in a sentence or in a preceding sentence that the pronoun has renamed. (For a detailed discussion on pronoun reference, see pages 115–18.)

Ant ◄─────── Pro
The gentleman bowed to *his* partner.

In order for a pronoun to function correctly, it must refer clearly to a well-defined antecedent, as in the example above. *His* can refer to only one noun in the sentence, *gentleman.* When a pronoun does not refer clearly to its antecedent, readers will be confused.

• If there are two possible antecedents for a pronoun in a sentence, rewrite the sentence so that the pronoun refers clearly to one of them.

AMBIGUOUS   Mr. Jones extended an invitation to Mr. Smith after *he* returned from *his* trip.
(What is the antecedent of *he/his?* Who has taken the trip?)

CLEAR   After *he* returned from *his* trip, Mr. Jones extended an invitation to Mr. Smith.
(Mr. Jones has taken the trip.)

AMBIGUOUS   Fran gave Julia *her* book on woodworking.
(What is the antecedent of *her?* Whose book is it?)

CLEAR   Fran found *her* book on woodworking and gave it to Julia.
(The book belongs to Fran.)

• The antecedent of a pronoun should be explicitly stated.

AMBIGUOUS   After the governor's announcement, *he* returned to the statehouse.
(It is impossible to tell if "governor" is the antecedent of *he*. In the example *governor's* is an adjective, not a noun.)

CLEAR   After the governor made his announcement, *he* returned to the statehouse.
(The antecedent of *he* is "governor.")

AMBIGUOUS   The office staff prepared furiously, but *it* came too soon.
(To what does *it* refer? The antecedent does not appear in the first clause.)

CLEAR   The office staff prepared furiously for the campaign, but *it* came too soon.
(The antecedent of *it* is "campaign.")

• The antecedent of the pronouns "it," "that," "this," and "which" should not have a broad reference.

AMBIGUOUS   I would enjoy climbing a mountain in the Himalayas or one of the towers in Manhattan. *It* would present an especially impressive challenge.
(The antecedent of *it* is too broad; the pronoun has no clear reference.)

CLEAR   I would enjoy climbing a mountain in the Himalayas or one of the towers in Manhattan. *Either* would present an especially impressive challenge.
(The pronoun "it" has been deleted; the pronoun "either" refers equally to a mountain or a tower.)

CLEAR   I would enjoy climbing a mountain in the Himalayas or one of the towers in Manhattan. A tower would present an especially impressive challenge.
(The reference to "one of the towers" is clearer since the pronoun "it" has been deleted.)

AMBIGUOUS   Frank has made several valuable suggestions
lately. *This* should be encouraged.
(The antecedent of *this* is too broad.)

CLEAR   Frank has made several valuable suggestions
lately. *This resourcefulness* should be encouraged.
(The noun "resourcefulness," which summarizes the content of a preceding clause, clarifies the meaning of the pronoun *this*.)

• The antecedent of "it," "you," and "they" should be clear and definite. Though the use of these indefinite pronouns is common in everyday speech (*"It* is raining." "New York City is where *they* serve the best deli sandwiches."), you should avoid using them in your writing.

FAULTY   On the floor of the Stock Exchange *they* trade stocks.

IMPROVED   On the floor of the Stock Exchange *brokers* trade stocks.

FAULTY   Expect *it* to rain daily in the tropics.

IMPROVED   Expect daily rainfall in the tropics.

• For the sake of clarity, a sentence should not contain both the pronoun "it" and the expletive "it."

FAULTY   *It* is helpful to keep a clear head in an emergency, but *it* is not always possible.
(The first *it* is an expletive. The second *it* is a pronoun.)

IMPROVED   To keep a clear head in an emergency is helpful, but *it* is not always possible.
(The expletive has been deleted. The pronoun *it* refers clearly to the subject of the preceding clause, "to keep . . . emergency.")

Improving the Clarity of Your Writing

Writing a grammatical sentence is no guarantee that you will communicate effectively, for grammatical sentences can be unclear. Once you are confident that your sentences are grammatical, examine your choice of words. Have you expressed yourself succinctly and precisely? Have you avoided using jargon that may obscure meaning? Have you refrained from overusing *to be* or *to have* as main verbs? In this chapter you will learn more about these subjects and in the process improve the clarity of your sentences.

WORDINESS

- Delete words, phrases, and clauses that do not add directly to the meaning of a sentence.

WORDY	Under all circumstances and in every case, always check the oil level in your car when you stop at a service station.
SUCCINCT	Always check the oil level in your car when you stop at a service station.
WORDY	When all is said and done, the purpose of having hobbies is to be relaxed, not obsessive.
SUCCINCT	The purpose of having hobbies is to be relaxed, not obsessive.

180

• Substitute one word for two words or more, when possible.

WORDY   Let's deal with this subject carefully.

SUCCINCT   Let's discuss this subject carefully.

WORDY   A reason to go to the voting booth is to add to the discussion of decisions that affect you.

SUCCINCT   Vote in order to participate in decisions that affect you.

WORDY   Why is it that some people do all of their best work in the morning and some people do all of their best work at night?

SUCCINCT   Why do some people work better in the morning than they do at night?

• Substitute a brief phrase for a lengthy phrase or clause.

WORDY   Ever since you took it upon yourself to leave, I have had trouble finding someone qualified enough to replace you.

SUCCINCT   Since you left, I have had trouble finding a qualified replacement.

WORDY   The basic reason I am writing this note is to say that I would very much like it if you were to consider coming back to your old position.

SUCCINCT   I am writing to ask that you consider returning to your old position.

Deleting or rewriting words, phrases, and clauses to eliminate wordiness made these sentences more concise. In each case, the clarity of the example improved with revision. Another way to avoid wordiness is to delete or to substitute pronouns for awkward repetitions.

• Avoid awkward repetitions.

A repeated word can be awkward if you have not intentionally used it as a stylistic device (see pages 192–94). Either rewrite the sentence(s) to delete a repetition, or use a substitute.

REPETITIOUS	Electric *typewriters* have become outdated with the development of word processors that do the work of *typewriters* more quickly and more accurately.
IMPROVED	Electric *typewriters* have become outdated with the development of word processors that do the *same work* more quickly and accurately.
REPETITIOUS	Word-processing programs allow *writers* to correct spelling mistakes and to shift the location of sentences without *the writer's* having to retype entire pages.
IMPROVED	Word-processing programs allow *writers* to correct spelling mistakes and to shift the location of sentences without having to retype entire pages.
REPETITIOUS	*Word processing* may prove to be the most used computer application in the home; *word processing* may also be the salvation of *students* who dislike writing because of the many drafts the *students'* teachers require.
IMPROVED	*Word processing* may prove to be the most used computer application in the home; *it* may also be the salvation of *students* who dislike writing because of the many drafts *their* teachers require.

Deleting repeated words or substituting pronouns for them improved the effectiveness of these sentences. Awkward repetitions can be difficult to spot while you're writing a letter, memorandum, or essay. So complete a draft of your work, and when you've finished, review what you've written with an eye for catching unplanned repetitions. Ideally, write two drafts, letting the first sit a few hours before beginning the second.

PRECISION

Precise writing is clear, accurate writing. Certain words are notoriously imprecise:

good   thing   bad   something   interesting

Evaluative terms such as "good" and "bad" may be your first critical response to a movie, book, or essay, but their descriptiveness is extremely limited. The person who wants to express himself precisely will qualify the meaning of these words. For instance, instead of saying, "This movie is good," you might say, more precisely:

> I enjoyed this movie because the main character was complex enough and her part was played well enough for me to recall my own young adulthood in a small, midwestern town.

To clarify your meaning, ask these exacting questions (as appropriate) of your subject:

Who?   What?   Where?   Why?   When?   How?

Instead of writing about a business or school report: "I don't like it," make your response more precise. Ask yourself: "What sections of the report didn't I like? Why? Are there parts of the report that are successful? Why are these parts successful, while others are not?" By asking such questions, you'll better understand your meaning, enabling you to clarify initially vague statements. For example, you might rewrite "I don't like it" as follows:

> In his report, Mr. Jones carefully documents each of his statements with statistics compiled from company records over the past five years. The report is well written but hardly goes far enough: it is a summary, not an analysis, and therefore does not satisfy our present needs.

JARGON

Jargon can be defined in two ways: as the specialized vocabulary of a professional or as an impressive-sounding but vague use of language. You should avoid jargon for two reasons: one, readers outside of your profession will probably not understand a specialized terminology; and two, your message will be obscured when you rely on overused phrases as a substitute for original thinking. Always choose your words carefully and know what they mean. Do not depend on phrases that add syllables but not substance.

The following example of political jargon was composed by a computer programmed to string together jargon-filled expressions spoken by politicians. The result is an impressive-sounding paragraph that actually says little. In this example, political jargon has taken the place of clear, precise thinking.

The international scene today is highly complex. In some ways, it is still a struggle between the free world and communism, for, despite all claims to the contrary, Russia is still a communist state. But, 1976 is not 1956. Russia has acquired nuclear and conventional military parity with us—and China and the Middle East make all dealings with the Russians more difficult. Therefore, in the day-to-day affairs of world politics, we must strive to manage and stabilize our relationships with other major powers. In a nuclear age, we can not escape the responsibility to build a safe future through wise diplomacy.

Jargon occurs with equal frequency in other fields. Here are two examples from business and sociology:

JARGON-FILLED   We employed a multi-systemed managerial-impact profile.

JARGON-FREE   We used a sophisticated test to analyze the effectiveness of our managers.

JARGON-FILLED	Semi-permanent diadic relationships provide the adolescent with the opportunities for experimentation that make for a more secure union in the third and fourth decades.
JARGON-FREE	Going steady when you're a teenager helps prepare you for marriage later on.

OVERUSE OF "TO BE" AND "TO HAVE"

Relying too heavily on forms of "to be" and "to have" as main verbs will diminish the effectiveness of your sentences. These words function well as auxiliaries, but as main verbs they lack force: they do not establish for a reader the clearest possible relationship between the subject of a sentence and its predicate. When possible, substitute a verb that more vividly expresses action than "to be" or "to have":

WEAK	Mrs. Smith *was* at the office door.
IMPROVED	Mrs. Smith *stood* at the office door.
WEAK	She *had* in her hands bonus checks for the engineers.
IMPROVED	She *held* in her hands bonus checks for the engineers.
WEAK	Peter Bagins, the project manager, *was* extremely happy to see her.
IMPROVED	Peter Bagins, the project manager, *rejoiced* at seeing her.

14

Improving the Style of Your Writing

You have seen in Chapters 12 and 13 how ungrammatical sentences and sentences lacking clarity can interfere with the process of communication. Another factor that impairs communication is ineffective style. Sentences can be grammatical and clearly written but at the same time cumbersome to read. Consider the following:

> His name was Robert McKenzie. He was born in Mason County, Virginia. His parents were from Kentucky. His parents arrived in Mason County in 1902. Robert McKenzie was born in 1902.

These sentences are perfectly clear and grammatical. Yet the prospect of reading twenty pages of such writing would wilt the hardiest soul, because the writing is stylistically flawed. *Style* can be defined as a quality of sentence structure and word choice that demonstrates a writer's sensitivity to the rhythms and richness of language. In this chapter you will learn various techniques for improving the style of your sentences, techniques that would enable you, for instance, to revise the example sentences above as follows:

> Robert McKenzie was born in Mason County, Virginia in 1902, the year his parents arrived from Kentucky.

To a certain extent, you are justified in thinking that stylistically pleasing sentences are a luxury. Certainly, the writer's first priority is to be grammatical and clear; and for many occasions, this will suffice. But if you wish to make a convincing presentation, then you should be interested in the stylistic success of your sentences. Be aware of the techniques at your disposal.

SENTENCE VARIETY

As shown in Chapter 5, there are four types of sentences: simple, compound, complex, and compound-complex. Effective writing usually includes a variety of sentence types. The obvious stylistic flaw of the example on page 186 ("His name was Robert . . .") is that every sentence is simple, creating a monotonous effect. Consider the stylistic problems of the following sentences. What revisions can you recommend?

> After the hurricane, relief agencies from the affected Gulf Coast states coordinated their efforts. Within hours, state officials offered medical aid to any family in need. When the storm passed, federal officials quickly appraised losses and offered low-interest loans.

Each sentence of the paragraph begins with a modifying phrase or clause, followed by a main clause, which makes the rhythm of the sentences essentially the same. The rhythm could be varied —and the paragraph improved—by revising any of the sentence structures. One revision might read as follows:

> After the hurricane, relief agencies from the affected Gulf Coast states coordinated their efforts. Within hours, state officials offered medical aid to any family in need, and federal officials quickly appraised losses and offered low-interest loans.

In this revision, the dependent clause "when the storm passed" was deleted because it was redundant. The combining of the second and third sentences with the coordinate conjunction "and" produced a parallel construction: "Within hours, state officials offered . . . and federal officials quickly appraised. . . ." Note that the meaning of the revised paragraph is identical to that of the original. When revising for style, you are interested in changing the presentation of a content, not the content itself.

PARALLELISM

Parallelism is a technique for eliminating awkward repetition and creating balance and emphasis in your writing. Whenever you use a coordinate or a correlative conjunction in a sentence, as in the example above, you create "slots" that should be filled by parallel, grammatically equivalent words.

John *rode* the bike and *fell* down.

Either *Alan* or *his father* should answer the phone.

One of the reasons that parallelism is such an effective stylistic tool is that it enables you to delete awkward repetitions. In the first example, the coordinate conjunction "and" allows you to use two verbs with one subject, "John."

John rode the bike. John fell down.

John *rode* the bike and *fell* down.

In the second example, the correlative conjunction "either/or" allows you to join two subjects with one verb, "answer."

Alan should answer the phone. His father should answer the phone.

Either *Alan* or *his father* should answer the phone.

In addition to nouns and verbs, other parts of speech can be made parallel. (You will notice in the following sentences how unparallel elements are awkward and should be revised.)

UNPARALLEL	The applicant was both *qualified* and *we found him interesting.*
PARALLEL ADJECTIVES	The applicant was both *qualified* and *interesting.*

UNPARALLEL   Sometime *after the game*
                              but *earlier than riding home,*
                              we lost Michael.

PARALLEL ADVERB PHRASES   Sometime *after the game*
                              but *before the ride home,* we
                              lost Michael.

Now that you've seen how parallelism works within sentences, you can apply its principles between sentences and between paragraphs.

• Use parallel elements in forming a series.

A series is a grouping of three or more grammatically parallel slots. Consider the following example:

Henry's car needed <u>Slot 1,</u> <u>Slot 2,</u> and <u>Slot 3</u>.

Each slot in the series must be filled with words that function as the same part of speech.

UNPARALLEL   Henry's car needed *a transmission, a water
                    pump,* and *the windshield was cracked.*

PARALLEL   Henry's car needed *a transmission, a water
                    pump,* and *a windshield.*

The construction of the first sentence is incorrect: the first two slots have been filled with an article and noun, and the third slot has been filled with an independent clause. The construction of the second sentence is correct: Slots 1, 2, and 3 each contain an article and noun, creating a well-balanced sentence.

• Use parallel elements within sentences, between sentences, and between paragraphs.

On the following page is an excerpt from John F. Kennedy's Inaugural Address, which contains numerous examples of parallelism. Through his use of parallel words, sentences, and paragraphs, Kennedy makes points forcefully and clearly.

PARALLEL ELEMENTS IN CONTEXT

Examine the uses of parallelism in the context of the following paragraphs from John F. Kennedy's Inaugural Address:

Let every nation know, whether it wishes us well or ill, that we shall pay any price, bear any burden, meet any hardship, support any friend, oppose any foe to assure the survival and the success of liberty.

This much we pledge—and more.

To those old allies whose cultural and spiritual origins we share, we pledge the loyalty of faithful friends. United, there is little we cannot do in a host of cooperative ventures. Divided, there is little we can do—for we dare not meet a powerful challenge split asunder.

To those new states whom we welcome to the ranks of the free, we pledge our word that one form of colonial control shall not have passed away merely to be replaced by a far more iron tyranny. We shall not always expect to find them supporting our view. But we shall always hope to find them strongly supporting their own freedom—and to remember that, in the past, those who foolishly sought power by riding the back of the tiger ended up inside.

ANALYSIS

PARALLELISM WITHIN SENTENCES:
Paragraph 1 is a single sentence containing parallel elements connected by a correlative conjunction (whether/or) and an implied coordinate conjunction (and):

WHETHER it wishes us *well* OR *ill*
Let every nation know that we shall

pay any price
bear any burden
meet any hardship
support any friend
(and)
oppose any foe

Each verb is identical
in its grammatical structure:

_____ any _____
Verb   Direct Object

PARALLELISM BETWEEN SENTENCES:
In paragraph 3, the second and third sentences are parallel:

United, there is little we cannot do. . . .
Divided, there is little we can do. . . .

In paragraph 4, the two final sentences share identical subjects and auxiliary verbs, and nearly identical adverbs.

PARALLELISM BETWEEN PARAGRAPHS:
Kennedy uses parallel sentences to address different listeners in paragraphs 3 and 4:

(Par. 3)   To those old allies whose cultural and spiritual origins we share, we pledge the loyalty of faithful friends.

(Par. 4)   To those new states whom we welcome to the ranks of the free, we pledge our word that. . . .

REPETITION

- Words, phrases, and clauses can be repeated intentionally in your writing to create emphasis. Unintentional repetition, by contrast, is usually awkward and should be avoided.

> UNINTENTIONAL REPETITION (AWKWARD)
> Mr. Randall could not *believe* that his clients *believed* he was insincere.

> INTENTIONAL REPETITION (EFFECTIVE)
> Many Americans now play state lotteries to make their *fortunes* —*fortunes* they feel can no longer be made through a life of hard work and dedication to an ideal.

Notice how the repeated word introduces a second clause that clarifies the meaning of *fortunes.*

- Instead of repeating a word to create emphasis, you might use a descriptive substitute, as long as it is similar in meaning to its antecedent and functions as the same part of speech.

> INTENTIONAL REPETITION
> We headed south along old Route 1—*the route* that we traveled a hundred times with our father when he hauled produce from the Carolinas.

> DESCRIPTIVE SUBSTITUTE
> We headed south along old Route 1—*a cracked, asphalt ribbon* that we traveled a hundred times with our father when he hauled produce from the Carolinas.

The advantage of using substitutes for creating emphasis is that they provide specific, descriptive information for the reader. Both "route" and "ribbon" are the same part of speech: noun. Notice, again, how the substitution/repetition is used to expand the meaning of the repeated word.

• Phrases and clauses, as well as single words, can be repeated within a sentence for emphasis and clarity.

COMPARE	Lifetimes of opportunities have been lost because so few people possess a spirit of adventure.
WITH	Lifetimes of opportunities have been lost, *dreamworlds have been squandered,* because so few people possess a spirit of adventure.

This second sentence is more emphatic than the first, because the opening clause, "Lifetimes of opportunities have been lost," is repeated and its meaning is clarified by the substitute "dreamworlds have been squandered."

COMPARE	In a larger sense, we cannot dedicate this ground.
WITH	In a larger sense, we cannot dedicate—*we cannot consecrate*—*we cannot hallow*—this ground. ABRAHAM LINCOLN

The repetition "we cannot" adds emphasis and power to Lincoln's words. Notice that these repetitions are grammatically parallel.

• Set apart repeated expressions in a sentence by using pairs of commas or dashes (unless the repetition occurs at the end of a sentence, in which case it is followed by a period):

> There are only two days this spring—*April 6 and May 21*—when I will be free to travel.
>
> OR
>
> There are only two days this spring, *April 6 and May 21,* when I will be free to travel.

Repetition Misused

Repetitions that are misused can make your sentences wordy and unnecessarily dramatic. While no simple formula can indicate whether repeating a word, phrase, or clause will be effective, bear in mind three questions that can be used as a guide:

1. Is the repetition helpful in organizing your sentence or paragraph?
2. Is the emphatic effect created by the repetition appropriate for your writing task?
3. In repeating or restating a sentence element, are you adding new and useful information?

If your answer to any of these is "no," then you should delete the repetitions in your sentence and express the same content in some other way. Unwarranted use of any stylistic technique reduces the effectiveness of your writing. Consider an example. If you were to summarize the events of a business meeting, would you use the following repetition?

Miss Jones called for suggestions—suggestions that might solve the problems raised by her personnel director.

The repetition of "suggestions" calls attention to itself unnecessarily and is overly dramatic for a simple report. Therefore, the second use of "suggestions" should be deleted and the sentence rewritten:

Miss Jones called for suggestions that might solve the problems raised by her personnel director.

PUNCTUATING FOR EFFECT

Dashes

Use a dash or dashes to create an emphatic pause in a sentence.

This we pledge—and more.

An effective job description—in addition to describing available employment—will also describe the emotional atmosphere of a workplace.

Colon

Place a colon at the end of an *independent* clause to make emphatic introductions:

> On hearing that he had fallen victim to a fatal disease while touring in Europe, Mark Twain wrote to an American newspaper: "Reports of my death are greatly exaggerated."
>
> The recent news from the boardroom could mean only one thing: a promotion.

A colon can be used to introduce a list (or series), in which case all items of the list must be grammatically parallel. A colon is incorrectly used when it does not follow an independent clause.

INCORRECT	The four months that have thirty days are: September, April, June, and November.
CORRECT	Four months have thirty days: September, April, June, and November.

ACTIVE- AND PASSIVE-VOICE SENTENCES

Sentences with transitive verbs can be arranged in two ways. In an active-voice sentence, the subject appears before the transitive verb and acts directly upon the object:

> Reggie kicked the ball.

In a passive-voice sentence, the order of the direct object and the subject is reversed, and the word "by" and a form of "to be" are added to the sentence:

> The ball was kicked by Reggie.

Often, "by" and the noun that follows are deleted from the passive-voice sentence:

> The ball was kicked.

• Use the active voice to stress the subjects of your sentences and to establish a direct, assertive quality in your writing.

The active voice stresses how a subject *performs* an action. The emphasis of a passive-voice sentence, by contrast, is on how an object *receives* an action. Since sentences in the passive voice emphasize the direct object—rather than the subject—they lack a direct, forceful quality:

> PASSIVE VOICE (AWKWARD)
> The bus was boarded by us at 1 P.M., and we were taken by the driver to the stadium, where we were welcomed by the mayor to the city's two-hundredth birthday party.
>
> ACTIVE VOICE (EFFECTIVE)
> We boarded the bus at 1 P.M. and went to the stadium, where the mayor welcomed us to the city's two-hundredth birthday party.

Notice how the active-voice sentence is more concise and more directly expressed than the passive-voice sentence.

- Use the passive voice when you wish to eliminate a redundant subject.

    Of the sentences below, the passive is preferable, since including the subject, "tobacco farmers," would be redundant:

> ACTIVE VOICE
> Tobacco farmers still grow a great deal of tobacco in Virginia.
>
> PASSIVE VOICE (PREFERABLE)
> A great deal of tobacco is still grown in Virginia.
> (The phrase "by tobacco farmers" is implied.)

- Use the passive voice when you want to remove awkward references to yourself from a sentence.

    Of the sentences below, the passive is preferable, since it allows the writer to avoid referring to himself/herself:

> ACTIVE VOICE
> I offer a more detailed discussion of the active and passive voices elsewhere in this book.
>
> PASSIVE VOICE
> A more detailed discussion of the active and passive voices is offered elsewhere in this book.
> (The phrase "by me" is implied.)

The passive-voice example on the preceding page illustrates how to emphasize the direct object of a sentence ("discussion") when the writer considers it to be more important than the original subject ("I"). For this reason, scientists, social scientists, and technical writers often use the passive voice in their writing.

PASSIVE VOICE

The flask was removed from the centrifuge, and its contents were placed under a microscope.

PASSIVE VOICE

The first step of the procedure is accomplished when the green light begins flashing.

Notice how the original subjects of these sentences are concealed by the passive voice.

PART FIVE

Paragraphs and Groups of Paragraphs

Organizing a Paragraph

A paragraph is a collection of sentences logically arranged and focused on a narrowly defined topic. Like sentences, paragraphs rarely occur in isolation. They are parts of larger units: the business letter or the memorandum or the essay for school. Learning about the composition of paragraphs is important in that the success of any larger form is entirely dependent on the success of its component parts. A letter will fail to communicate, for instance, if any of its paragraphs is poorly structured or poorly developed.

The sections that follow provide guidelines for writing paragraphs that will clearly and effectively express your ideas. At the same time, these sections will prepare you for the discussion in Chapter 16 on organizing groups of paragraphs. Chapters 15 and 16 are closely related, because the principles of organization that apply to sentences vis-à-vis a paragraph also apply to paragraphs vis-à-vis an entire essay. As you will see, both paragraphs and larger forms (letters, essays) should be *unified* and *coherent*. Their parts should be *arranged* carefully, according to a plan; and their ideas should be *developed* thoroughly. A parallel can also be drawn between the term *topic sentence,* which is unique to paragraphs, and the term *thesis statement,* which is unique to larger forms.

On page 225 you will find a chapter summary in the form of a checklist; use the questions from the list to evaluate the effectiveness of your paragraphs.

THE TOPIC SENTENCE

A topic sentence has two functions: it narrowly defines the topic of a paragraph, and it makes an assertion or claim about that topic. Ideally, a topic sentence should be just broad enough to allow for a focused, five-to-ten (sometimes more) sentence discussion. A writer controls the level of generality of a topic sentence by renaming or modifying its subject, and by making more or less specific claims about that subject in the predicate.

Limiting the Topic Sentence

Each of the following sentences has a subject and a predicate. Which sentence would make the best topic sentence?

1. Various foods take differing times to prepare and to cook.
2. Chinese food is more difficult to prepare than to cook.
3. Mushrooms take ten minutes to slice and twenty seconds to cook.

The second sentence would make the most effective topic sentence. Let's examine why.

The subject of sentence 1 is too broad to be useful as the organizing sentence of a paragraph, for "various foods" could include any or all cuisines of the world. The predicate "take differing times to prepare and to cook" does not help to limit the subject in any way. The sentence might be appropriate for organizing an entire book, but it is not nearly specific enough for organizing a single paragraph. Let's examine sentence 3:

Mushrooms take ten minutes to slice and twenty seconds to cook.

This sentence, by contrast, is *too* narrowly defined to be useful as a topic sentence. The subject, mushrooms, is more specific than "various foods" and would be appropriate as the topic of a paragraph, since there is a great deal one can write about mushrooms (how they're grown, their nutritional value, their shelf life, and so on). However, the predicate of this sentence—*take ten minutes to slice and twenty seconds to cook*—so narrowly limits the subject "mushrooms" that there is little left to discuss. The sentence would be effective as a detail or an example used in another paragraph—perhaps one organized with sentence 2 as its topic sentence:

Chinese food is more difficult to prepare than to cook.

Both the subject and the predicate of this sentence are broad enough, but not too broad, to be the topic sentence of a paragraph. "Chinese food," like "mushrooms," is narrower in focus than the subject of the first example, "various foods." (Notice that "Chinese" is a more precise adjective than "various.") Unlike the predicate from sentence 3, the predicate of this sentence—*is more difficult to prepare than to cook*—is broad enough to allow for an additional, detailed discussion. The predicate limits, but does not too narrowly limit, the subject, and the result is a topic sentence that could focus the discussion of a paragraph on the relative difficulties of preparing and cooking Chinese food.

Here are three observations about topic sentences and the parts that constitute them:

1. The topic sentence most desirable for organizing a paragraph is the one that is neither too general nor too specific.
2. The subject of a topic sentence can be focused or limited by using modifiers and narrowly defined nouns.
3. The subject can be focused or limited by the predicate of the sentence, which makes a specific assertion about the subject.

Use topic sentences as an aid in organizing your writing. When you properly focus a topic sentence, you have a solid basis upon which to include or exclude information as you write a paragraph. A good topic sentence also enables the reader to anticipate the contents of a paragraph and thus be better able to follow your presentation as you make it. For example, consider two topic sentences and the inferences one can draw from them:

TOPIC SENTENCE   John Stuart Mill, a prominent nineteenth-century philosopher, had been a celebrated child prodigy.

SUBJECT   John Stuart Mill

PREDICATE   had been a celebrated child prodigy

(The likely content of the paragraph would be a listing of Mill's startling accomplishments as a child.)

TOPIC SENTENCE   A glimpse into the twenty-first century would reveal some startling possibilities for mass transportation.

SUBJECT   a glimpse into the twenty-first century

PREDICATE   would reveal some startling possibilities for mass transportation

(The likely content of the paragraph would be a discussion of specific forms of mass transit in the future.)

Placement of the Topic Sentence

The most direct and most common method for organizing a paragraph is to place its topic sentence first.* This is known as a *deductive arrangement,* in which the most general statement of the paragraph precedes the details that support it.

A glimpse into the twenty-first century would reveal some startling possibilities for mass transportation. At a scientific conference held in November of 1966, scientists reported exciting developments in underground transportation making use of nuclear power. Electric automobiles that could be recharged overnight in home garages were viewed as the car of the future for taking the family to the supermarket and for other around-town chores. The suburban commuter, it was felt, would, in addition, rent an inexpensive electric car from the railroad to take him from his home to the commuting station. He would leave the car at the station until he returned from work and would pick up a similar one in which to make his way back home. Torpedo-like trains that fly

*The topic sentences of paragraphs here and throughout the chapter will be underlined.

underground and airbuses that take off vertically are all part of the transportation vision of the future.   GERALD LEINWAND

By contrast, observe an *inductively arranged* paragraph, in which the most general statement, the topic sentence, is placed last:

> You have watched films of their adoring fans, crying, cheering, clawing for scraps of clothing. One photograph in *Life* immortalized a young woman with a tuft of grass in her hand and tears streaming down her face: "Ringo walked here," she sobbed. Their long hair insulted many adults but became a symbol of protest for a generation. Likewise, their music offended but became a cultural touchstone for millions. <u>Twenty years ago, the Beatles arrived in New York and stirred the emotions of young and old alike.</u>

An inductive arrangement is effective when you want to lead a reader through the process of thinking that resulted in your topic sentence. Placing the topic sentence last can also create suspense in a paragraph: as readers learn more about the topic with each sentence, they wonder where you are leading them. In business letters and memoranda, the inductive technique works well if you have unhappy news for your reader, for you'll be able to build up to your main point slowly. By the time your reader gets to the conclusion, he or she will already have anticipated it.

Sometimes, stating a topic sentence is too obvious or heavy-handed for a paragraph; in that case, the topic sentence should be deleted. Paragraphs with implied topic sentences are relatively rare, however. When they do occur, they are organized as carefully as paragraphs whose topic sentences are explicitly stated:

> The [Chesapeake Bay] produces 33 percent of the U.S. oyster catch, and 50 percent of its tasty blue crabs; not long ago, the bay also supplied 6 million pounds of striped bass annually (on bay waters the species is known as "rockfish"). But over the past decade, the catch of prized striped bass has plummeted by 90 percent to a mere 600,000 pounds; ominously for the future, current counts of young striped bass are at record lows. Another cause of great concern: the bay's recent oyster catches of 1.1 million pounds are just one third the sumptuous averages of 30 years ago.   WILLIAM MCCLUSKEY

Though not stated, the topic sentence of this paragraph is clearly understood: <u>What was once a rich and varied marine life in the Chesapeake Bay is now endangered.</u> Notice that the discussion in the paragraph is focused on a single topic, as though the topic sentence had been explicitly stated.

Topic sentences may be placed anywhere in a paragraph, provided you have a good reason for so placing them. The topic sentence at the beginning or end of a paragraph is the most common arrangement, but there are others that work as well—such as the second or third sentence following an introductory remark. The material you are presenting will help determine the most suitable location.

UNITY

Unity is achieved when every sentence of a paragraph refers directly to the topic sentence. A unified paragraph is one that contains no extraneous information. Pictorially, such a paragraph can be represented as follows:

Let's examine one well-structured paragraph:

<u>It was about this time I conceived the bold and arduous project of arriving at moral perfection.</u> I wished to live without committing any fault at any time; I would conquer all that either natural inclination, custom, or company might lead me into. As I knew, or thought I knew, what was right and wrong, I did not see why I might not always do the one and avoid the other. But I soon

found I had undertaken a task of more difficulty than I had imagined. While my care was employed in guarding against one fault, I was often surprised by another; habit took the advantage of inattention; inclination was sometimes too strong for reason. I concluded, at length, that the mere speculative conviction that it was our interest to be completely virtuous was not sufficient to prevent our slipping, and that the contrary habits must be broken, and good ones acquired and established, before we can have any dependence on a steady, uniform rectitude of conduct. For this purpose I therefore contrived the following method.

BENJAMIN FRANKLIN

This paragraph from Franklin's *Autobiography* is unified: the content of every sentence is directly related to the topic sentence:

1. Topic sentence: "It was about this time I conceived the bold and arduous project of arriving at moral perfection."
2. "I wished to live without committing any fault."
3. "I would conquer all" vice.
4. "I knew . . . what was right and wrong."
5. "I had undertaken a task."
6. While I was "guarding against one fault," others surprised me.
7. Merely speculating about virtue is not enough.

To achieve paragraph unity, identify the topic sentence; summarize the remaining sentences in the paragraph, as above; and determine whether the content of each refers to the topic sentence. Every sentence should contain some word or phrase directly related to the topic, if the paragraph is to be unified.

COHERENCE

A paragraph is coherent if the relationship *among* its sentences is clear. A writer should examine every sentence in relation to the others, asking of each: *How* does this sentence follow logically from the preceding sentence and lead logically to the next? Unless you can justify the location of every sentence within the paragraph, you risk incoherence.

Pictorially, a coherent paragraph can be represented as follows. The arrows leading from one sentence to the next indicate that the relationship among sentences is clear and direct.

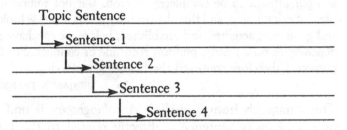

Conceivably, a paragraph could be unified—every sentence could refer to a topic sentence—but still be incoherent:

> The *Titanic* was widely publicized as the safest and most modern of luxury liners. She was famed for her sumptuous ballrooms and elegant restaurants. Designers assured passengers that the heavy steel hull could not be punctured. The decor of her staterooms rivaled that of the finest hotels of Europe. Every possible safety precaution had been taken in her design.

The topic sentence of this paragraph is clear, and the content of each sentence that follows is related to the main topic. However, no apparent logic links one sentence with another, and the paragraph is incoherent. By contrast, examine a paragraph that *is* coherent. Notice how the author uses *pronouns, conjunctions, parallel structures,* and *repeated words* to link sentences so that the logical relationships among them are apparent.

EXAMINING PARAGRAPH COHERENCE

Examine the relationship among sentences in the following paragraph:

¹Mechanical devices are not responsible for the safety or accident on any job; the human who operates machines, of a simple or a complex nature, is responsible for the operation of the

machine. [2]He is safe with the machine if he is safety conscious, if he is careful, and if he understands the right way to do his job. [3]The most effective safety program then must be based upon the attitude of the workman. [4]If the workman recognizes that safety and carefulness are his job, then his job will be a safe one. [5]If the workman will not recognize the importance of safety, if his attitude is one of risk rather than safety, then no amount of rules will make his job anything but a risky one. [6]What has been said in the jest about automobile safety is applicable to all kinds of safety: "The most important part of an automobile is the *nut* at the wheel." [7]Machines, hammers, saws, scaffolds and nails are dumb and have no intelligence of their own: only the man who directs them can make them do whatever job they are designed for. [8]However, it is well to remember that all tools are potentially weapons and potentially dangerous; if the workman will be safety conscious and careful they will be tools to build, but if he fails they will be weapons that do harm.

Reprinted by permission of American Technical Publishers, Inc.

ANALYSIS

Sentence 1:
This is the topic sentence of the paragraph.

Sentence 2:
The pronoun "he" repeats the subject of the preceding clause. "Safe," "safety," and "machine" similarly link sentence 2 to sentence 1.

Sentence 3:
"Safety program" refers the reader to sentence 2. The conjunction "then" invites the reader to summarize the logical development of sentences 1 and 2 (about worker safety) and to accept the logical conclusion of sentence 3 (that safety "must be based upon the attitude of the workman").

Sentences 4 and 5:
Both sentences are structured around parallel "if . . . then" clauses. The words "safety," "carefulness," "job," "attitude," and "workman" appear in preceding sentences in the paragraph.

Sentence 6:
This anecdote pertains to the topic of safety. The relationship between this sentence and the others might have been strained had the author not repeated the word "safety."

Sentence 7:
Here the author interprets the anecdote of sentence 6. In the process, he restates and expands the topic sentence (sentence 1).

Sentence 8:
"However," placed at the beginning of the clause, establishes a contrast with the preceding clause. "Tools" in this sentence repeats, by summarizing in one word, the list of particular tools in the preceding sentence.

To achieve paragraph coherence, use the following techniques to establish logical connections among sentences:

- Repeat words and use pronouns to establish that one subject remains under discussion. (See pages 192–3.)
- Use conjunctions to establish specific logical relationships among sentences. (See pages 28–34.)
- Use parallel phrases and clauses to enable readers to anticipate your content. (See pages 188–9.)

Having written a paragraph and having made certain that all of its sentences pertain to one narrowly defined topic, you should examine the relationship among the sentences themselves. Can you justify the location of every sentence in the paragraph? Can you explain how each sentence follows logically from the preceding sentence and leads logically to the next? If your paragraphs are to be coherent, you must be able to answer these questions with an unqualified *yes*.

ARRANGEMENT

A paragraph is composed of a topic sentence (either stated or implied) and sentences that expand upon that topic. As a general principle, the sentences of a paragraph should be arranged according to an easily recognizable pattern. Among the most common are the spatial, chronological, and topical patterns.

Spatial Arrangement

The sentences of a paragraph can be arranged spatially by drawing the reader's attention to objects or people in terms of their physical proximity to one another. It is important that the order of presentation be simple: from left to right, top to bottom, east to west, north to south, outer to inner, near to far, and so on. A writer may choose to reverse or combine these orderings, as long as the organization of the paragraph remains clear.

> The layout of Robert's apartment is convenient. When you open the door, you're standing in a hallway. The light switches are immediately to your left. On your right, just beyond the closet, is the bathroom; just beyond that, a few feet down the hall, is the kitchen. The two bedrooms are opposite the kitchen, on the left. Beyond the bedrooms, at the end of the hallway, are the living and dining rooms.

In this paragraph, the writer walks the reader through an apartment—down a hallway, observing the location of rooms on either side. (The dominant arrangement of details is near to far.) Notice that the spatial relationship among rooms is clear enough for the reader to draw a rough map. Any spatially arranged paragraph should achieve at least this level of detail.

Chronological Arrangement

In a chronological arrangement, the writer organizes information by time, proceeding from an early period to a later one, or vice versa. Transitions commonly used in chronological arrangements include *once; first, second, etc.; then; next; earlier;* and *later.*

> Freedom of speech, as embodied in the First Amendment to the United States Constitution, has origins dating back to other forms of government: the participatory democracy of Greece's city states; the later development of Roman codes and institutions based on a "universal natural law," where all men were seen as equal; the still later Magna Charta of 1215; the Edict of Nantes (1598); France's Declaration of the Rights of Man and the Citizen (1789); as well as our own Constitution with its first ten amendments. These all represent tumultuous milestones in the development of our free society.   VICTOR CLINE

Cline's phrase, "has origins dating back to," in the topic sentence prepares the reader for a chronological arrangement of material. His earliest point of reference in the chronology is the participatory democracies of Greece. Then, combining transitional techniques such as "later" and "still later," he takes us forward through history. Since a third use of *later* would be repetitious, Cline switches to ordering events by citing years, which he places in parentheses. His mixing of transitions is typical of effective chronological arrangements.

Topical Arrangement

If you are not treating the topic of a paragraph spatially or chronologically, then you will most likely treat it topically. The term *topical arrangement* is a general category which includes several techniques for ordering sentences. Four common techniques follow:

1. Present the topic's component parts and discuss each. (For example, the mechanism of a clock could be discussed in terms of its component parts.)
2. Organize sentences in ascending or descending order of importance. (For example, a collection of stamps might be presented in terms of least to most valuable, or vice versa.)

3. Discuss the attractive—or unattractive—features of the topic. (For example, the proposed solution to a problem could be reviewed in light of its attractive or unattractive features; an object, such as an automobile, could be similarly reviewed.)
4. Discuss the functions of the topic. (For example, any tool or utensil could be discussed in terms of its function.)

When arranging the sentences of a paragraph topically, you should be able to justify your method of arrangement and the location of every sentence within that arrangement. For instance, if you were discussing the functions of a gardening hoe, which would you discuss first? second? third? Why?

DEVELOPMENT

Thus far we have reviewed four important components of the effective paragraph: the topic sentence, unity, coherence, and arrangement. The fifth, and final, component discussed in this chapter is *development.* It is important for you as a writer to develop the ideas and information expressed in your paragraphs carefully and thoroughly. In this section you will learn six techniques for doing so.

Definition

In attempting to define an object, idea, or emotion, you seek to clarify the qualities that distinguish it from others of its kind. Depending on the complexity of your definition, you may need to write one line or several paragraphs. For lengthy definitions, isolate the components of that which is being defined and treat a few—or perhaps one—per paragraph. Whether you are writing a simple or a complex definition, make certain that you do the following:

1. Name the object, idea, or emotion that you will be defining.
2. Explain each aspect of your definition thoroughly and unambiguously.

A single, or primary, rainbow has red on the outside, violet inside. Its arc, 40 degrees in radius, is always on a line with the observer and the sun. When you see a bow, the sun is behind you. Sometimes a secondary rainbow forms outside the primary. It is fainter, with colors reversed—red inside, violet outside. The secondary bow forms from light reflected twice within drops. Light may be reflected more than twice, so occasionally up to five bows are seen. Another type of bow—red, or red and green—may appear with primary and secondary bows.

HERBERT S. ZIM and ROBERT H. BAKER

Note: The topic sentence of this paragraph is implied, not stated: <u>Single and multiple rainbows have distinct characteristics and occur due to differing natural conditions.</u>

Process

A *process* is a systematic presentation of the steps involved in achieving some result. You could describe the process of making a cake; of becoming a civil servant; of learning to relax. Whatever your subject, the steps of the process must be arranged systematically (and often chronologically) in order to be useful.

<u>Though there are chefs whose omelettes are works of art, basic omelette making is a skill that can be learned by any veteran of the kitchen.</u> First, it should "be noted that thirty seconds beating with the fork is enough . . . to 'confuse' six eggs. Three teaspoons of cold water added to them makes the omelette tender, whereas milk has the opposite effect. The pan should heat gradually on a medium hot fire, never too quickly nor to excess. Test its temperature with a bit of butter on the end of a fork. The butter should definitely sizzle but *not* turn brown. A generous tablespoon is adequate for a six-egg omelette. Spread it by tilting and turning the pan in all directions to coat the surface. When the frothing bubbles of butter have subsided, in go your eggs. Stir just a second or two with the *flat* of the fork. Tilt the pan to run the eggs up and around the sides, and keep the pan moving in a back and forth motion so the omelette remains slipping and free. Lift the edges here and there and allow the liquid part to run under . . . Fold the omelette simply with a spatula, left side to center, while the surface of the eggs is still soft. Then with the right side slipping

over the edge of the pan, hold the platter until it is in close contact and turn the pan completely over, thus accomplishing the third fold neatly."   NARCISSA CHAMBERLAIN*

The main clause of the topic sentence, "basic omelette . . . kitchen," signals that a process will follow. The next sentence begins the process with the word "first." This paragraph is arranged chronologically, in the order that steps must be taken to make a good omelette. When appropriate, the author explains in detail an important step in the process—in this case, heating the pan. Also notice the use of transitional words common to chronological arrangements—*when* and *then*—which begin two separate sentences.

Cause and Effect

When you need to explain or comment on the results of some action or behavior, a paragraph organized by cause and effect works well. Often, explanations are complex and lengthy, because proving causation—that one event is directly responsible for a certain result—is difficult. Most real-life situations contain enough variables to complicate any cause-and-effect analysis. For instance, if your car's engine failed thirty minutes after you filled the gas tank at a certain station, would you be justified in claiming that the gasoline was fouled and caused your engine to fail? To do so, you'd have to take into account such variables as the condition of the engine before you filled the tank; the level and condition of the oil; the frequency of having your car serviced; and an analysis of the gasoline in your tank (to see whether water was present). Only after you have considered many possible explanations and accounted for a wide range of variables can you claim with confidence that a cause-and-effect analysis is accurate.

Though you should always be sensitive to complexity when developing a cause-and-effect analysis, there are cases in which the relationship is straightforward and the presentation brief enough to offer in a paragraph.

*From *The Omelette Book,* by Narcissa Chamberlain. Copyright © 1955 by Narcissa Chamberlain. Reprinted by permission of Alfred A. Knopf, Inc.

After its thickness, the *shape* of a sleeping bag can have a lot to do with its warmth and weight. Larger bags are roomier—but, like bigger houses, they need more insulation (or hotter heaters) to keep their occupants warm. Because *you* are the heater, you will need more insulation thickness in a larger bag than in a closer-fitting one. Hence, not only must you carry more weight just because the bag is bigger, but you carry more weight because the insulation must be thicker too.   MIKE SCHERER

In this cause-and-effect discussion, the author claims that the size and shape of a sleeping bag are directly related to (i.e., causally connected with) the warmth and weight of the bag. As in any effective cause-and-effect discussion, the author provides clear and explicit reasoning for his conclusion—that the result of manufacturing a large sleeping bag is to increase the weight of the bag and the thickness of its insulation.

There are several transitions commonly used in the cause-and-effect paragraph: *since, because, so, if, then, therefore, thus,* and *hence.* Each establishes a causal relationship between sentences or between elements within a sentence.

Examples

A common technique for developing paragraphs is to provide examples of a general statement (which frequently turns out to be the topic sentence). Examples are a crucial form of evidence that writers use to support their claims. If, for instance, you wrote, "The councilwoman from my district is the most active member of the city government," no one would have reason to agree unless you provided examples, specific instances that would document your claim. But what if you had a hundred examples and were making the claim in a letter to the editor of your local paper? Would you use all of your examples? Not likely. You would want to choose examples judiciously, using only the most vivid. A few well-chosen examples are sufficient to support the points you wish to make.

If you have several examples that demonstrate a particular statement, your method of arranging them must be clear. Which example will you place first? second? third? Will you number examples? Arrangement according to ascending or descending order of importance is common; so is a chronological arrangement (as in the example paragraph below). *For instance, for example,* and *namely* are the most frequently used expressions for introducing examples. (The Latin abbreviation *e.g.* means for example.)

> Various explanations of human uniqueness have been offered and later rejected. "One, dating back to Benjamin Franklin, stated that humans were the only tool-using animals. But numerous kinds of animals employ tools, among them the California sea otter, which carries a stone under water with which to pound mollusks loose from rocks. So the definition was revised . . . again, this time to identify humans as the only tool-*making* animals. That one lasted for decades, until chimpanzees living under natural conditions were observed to make tools. Most recently, language has been fastened upon as the single, uniquely diagnostic trait for humankind. For the time being at least, it appears to be a valid distinction, even though in recent years several chimpanzees have been trained in laboratories to communicate by the use of American Sign Language, by arranging plastic disks, and by pushing buttons on a computerized control board."   PETER FARB

This paragraph contains three examples of the claim made in the topic sentence, that various explanations of human uniqueness have been offered and rejected:

1. Use of tools—rejected because sea otters use tools;
2. Creation of tools—rejected because chimpanzees create tools;
3. Use of language—challenged because chimpanzees have been taught sign language.

Like any well-written paragraph, this one follows an easily accessible logic, one indication of which is Farb's smooth, effective use of transitions (a subtle version of a numbering system, used to arrange examples chronologically). Farb's paragraph is effective because his presentation is systematic but not mechanical.

> One [definition], dating back to Benjamin Franklin, stated . . . So the definition was revised again, this time . . . Most recently, . . . For the time being, at least, . . .

Comparison/Contrast

A comparison is a discussion of similarities, and a contrast a discussion of differences, between two or more people, places, or things. Such a discussion encourages you to focus on details that illuminate the people, items, etc., being compared. For example, if you were debating which of two brands of gloves to buy, you might compare the prices, the stitching, and the insulation. Based on these separate comparisons, you'd gain specific information about the gloves and then make your choice.

Notice that a comparative analysis makes sense only when you compare elements of the same substance or type. A comparison of the insulation of one glove with the stitching of the other glove would lead to no useful conclusion. Categories of comparison should also be significant. Why spend your time comparing the printing on the labels of the gloves? Choose categories for comparison that will allow you to make meaningful observations.

There are two principal ways of structuring a comparison and contrast.

METHOD 1 (SUMMARY APPROACH)
Topic sentence
Summary of A's (i.e., the first person's, place's, or thing's) significant features
Summary of B's significant features
Comparisons of A and B
Contrasts of A and B
Optional: At the end of the paragraph, repeat the claim made in the topic sentence.

METHOD 2 (ELEMENT-BY-ELEMENT APPROACH)
Topic sentence
Significant feature 1
   Compare and contrast A and B with respect to feature 1.
Significant feature 2
   Compare and contrast A and B with respect to feature 2.
Significant feature 3 and so on
Optional: At the end of the paragraph, repeat the claim made in the topic sentence.

The structure you choose for your comparison and contrast will depend upon your writing task. Generally, the summary approach works best with brief discussions; the element-by-element approach, with lengthier, more complex discussions. There are a number of transitions commonly used to establish contrasts:

although	however	while
but	others	yet
by contrast	some	on the one hand
even though	whereas	on the other hand

The transitions "while," "even though," "although," and "whereas" are subordinate conjunctions that establish a contrast *within* a sentence:

> *Whereas* Ms. Jones believes that all new employees should enroll in special orientation classes, Mr. Thompson believes that they can learn whatever they need to on the job.

The other transitions establish a contrast *between* sentences:

> Ms. Jones believes that all new employees should enroll in special orientation classes; *however*, Mr. Thompson believes that they can learn whatever they need to on the job.

Four transitions are used to establish a comparison:

and	also
as well	similarly

In the following example, observe the author's use of transitions. What structure has he chosen to organize his paragraph?

> Wine, like a human being, is born, passes through adolescence, matures, grows old, and, if not drunk in time, becomes senile and finally dies. Its life span, like that of man, is unpredictable at the time of birth. It suffers from maladies to which some succumb while others recover. Some wines are aristocrats, some plebeians, but the mass of wines are just sturdy, honest, good fellows. Yet all are interesting, more so as one gets to know them better, because no two vintages of the same wine, or any two wines, are ever identical. Each has its own individuality. There will be family

resemblances and characteristics which can be recognized quite readily, but the more one studies the subject and notes these intriguing differences, the greater will be the enjoyment from wines.   HAROLD J. GROSSMAN

Grossman uses the element-by-element technique for organizing his comparison between wine and human beings, which he compares along a number of their dimensions: aging, unpredictability, maladies, individuality, and family resemblances. Notice how these criteria for comparison are developed from a central analogy—"wine is like a human being"—to organize the paragraph and illuminate the object under analysis. With this analogy, the author has chosen to explore comparisons. (In every sentence, we find a likeness between wines and people.) The analogy also enables the author to observe differences among wines (inasmuch as there are differences among people—i.e., some are "aristocrats," some are "plebeians," etc.).

Description

A description is a re-creation, in words, of some object, person, place, emotion, or sensation. This re-creation is accomplished when the writer divides a subject into its component parts and then offers a detailed account of these parts, presenting them to the reader in some clear and orderly fashion. As a sales representative, you would want to describe products in vivid and appealing detail. As a reporter, your job might be to describe an event—when, where, and how it took place. As a scientist, you would observe the conditions of an experiment and record them for review by others.

However small a part it may play in a letter or report, a description can have a disproportionately large impact on the overall effectiveness of your writing. In order to make your descriptions effective, use vivid detail. Answer as many of the following questions about your subject as you think appropriate: *who, what, when, where,* and *how.* (The question *why* leads to a discussion of cause and effect.) Answering these questions will involve an appeal to one or more of the senses: sight, sound, smell, taste, and touch. *Consciously choose your point of view and perspective when writing a description and avoid shifts in either.* Perspective denotes the physical relationship of a person to the object he or she is describing. For instance, one could describe the Empire State Building from the outside, the inside, the top, the bottom, etc. Shifts in perspective can be disorienting: if in describing a house you focused on the exterior and then abruptly shifted to a description of the kitchen stove, you'd risk confusing your reader.

Point of view denotes the psychological relationship of a person to the object he or she is describing. *What we see* depends to a great extent on *the way we see.* A geologist, a poet, and a rock climber, all looking at Mont Blanc, would offer differing descriptions of the mountain, based on their distinct points of view, their ways of seeing the world. Shifts in an author's point of view within a description can be disorienting: if while inspecting an apartment complex for structural flaws you turned to the owner and said, "I really don't like the color of the curtains in the main lobby," you'd doubtless confuse that person—for you'd be shifting points of view from professional to personal.

Avoid unnecessary shifts in point of view and perspective. If the logic of a paragraph requires a shift, then announce it with an appropriate transition.

Consider the following three descriptions. The points of view, the perspectives, and the intended audiences differ. Yet, observe the similarities: each author describes an object by examining its component parts in vivid, precise detail; each arranges these parts in a clear and orderly fashion; and each maintains a consistent (albeit unique) point of view and perspective.

DESCRIPTION 1

During the second month, the embryo increases in mass about 500 times. By the end of this period, it weighs about $\frac{1}{30}$ ounce, slightly less than the weight of an aspirin tablet, and is about 1 inch long. Despite its small size, it is almost human-looking and, after two months, is generally referred to as a fetus. Its head is still relatively large because of the early and rapid development of the brain, but the head size will continue to be reduced in proportion to body size throughout gestation (and through childhood as well). Arms, legs, elbows, knees, fingers and toes are all forming during this time, and as another reminder of our ancestry, there is a temporary tail. The tail reaches its greatest length in the second month and then gradually begins to disappear; it is entirely gone in 94 percent of all babies by the time they are born (of this 6 percent, the tail is generally detectable only by x-ray). Liver, gallbladder, and pancreas are present, and there is clear differentiation of the divisions of the intestinal tract. The liver now constitutes about 10 percent of the body of the fetus and is its main blood-forming organ.   HELEN CURTIS

This description of a human embryo was written by a biologist, who remains consistent both in perspective and point of view throughout the paragraph. Note the objective tone; the precise, quantified descriptions; and the topical arrangement.

DESCRIPTION 2

The Filamatic Air-Wash Container Cleaner will automatically remove loose dirt, dust, carton lint, fine glass particles, and other foreign matter from glass, metal, or plastic containers. The Air-Wash Container Cleaner operates by the simultaneous application of high-pressure compressed air and vacuum. High-pressure air jets dislodge the particles from the interior surface of the container and keep them in suspension, while a vacuum extracts the foreign matter for deposit into a storage tank. Nothing is expelled into the atmosphere.

This description was written by an advertiser whose job it was to define and precisely describe the operation of an industrial product. The description explains *what* this product is and *how* it works. Note the precise detail: as a customer reading this advertisement, you would know exactly what to expect on ordering an Air-Wash Container Cleaner. As with the earlier example, the author remains consistent in both perspective and point of view.

DESCRIPTION 3

"Thunderbolts"—that ridiculous word ought to be changed—
but nevertheless the thing "love at first sight" does exist. I remember the charming and noble Wilhelmina, despair of the beaux of
Berlin; she scorned love and laughed at its follies. Her youth, wit,
and beauty dazzled the eye, as did her happiness in every way.
Boundless wealth, in giving her full scope to develop her qualities,
seemed to conspire with nature to show the world a rare example
of perfect happiness in a person who perfectly deserved it. She was
twenty-three, and had been at court long enough to have rejected
the homage of the greatest in the realm. She was held up as a
paragon of modest but unshakable virtue; even the most eligible
began to despair of ever pleasing her, and aspired only to win her
friendship. One night she went to a ball at Prince Ferdinand's,
and danced for ten minutes with a young captain.   STENDHAL

This evocative description of a young woman serves as an
example of Stendhal's introductory claim—that the phenomenon
"love at first sight" exists. Stendhal uses vivid detail to make
Wilhelmina appear unapproachable, preparing us for the eventual
thunderbolt of love. With the paragraph's last line, "One night
she . . . danced for ten minutes with a young captain," our
curiosity is pricked. We know that the description of Wilhelmina
must be successful; otherwise, we would not be interested in
learning what happens next. Note Stendhal's point of view as an
observer who sees not only physical attributes, but psychological
and social ones as well.

As different as the above three examples are in subject, in
perspective, and in point of view, they nonetheless share the
qualities that make descriptions effective. The author of each
passage divides his or her subject into component parts and then
presents a detailed, vivid account of these parts in a clear and
orderly fashion.

PARAGRAPHS WITH MULTIPLE STRUCTURES

Paragraphs need not follow a single arrangement or a single method of development. As long as you control the organization of your sentences and are confident that readers will understand your meaning, then you should feel justified in combining techniques. Consider the following paragraph:

> Despite the name "sibling rivalry," this miserable passion has only incidentally to do with a child's actual brothers and sisters. The real source of it is the child's feelings about his parents. When a child's older brother or sister is more competent than he, this arouses only temporary feelings of jealousy. Another child being given special attention becomes an insult only if the child fears that, in contrast, he is thought little of by his parents, or feels rejected by them. It is because of such an anxiety that one or all of a child's sisters or brothers may become a thorn in his flesh. Fearing that in comparison to them he cannot win his parents' love and esteem is what inflames sibling rivalry. This is indicated in stories by the fact that it matters little whether the siblings actually possess greater competence. The Biblical story of Joseph tells that it is jealousy of parental affection lavished on him which accounts for the destructive behavior of his brothers. Unlike Cinderella's, Joseph's parent does not participate in degrading him, and, on the contrary, prefers him to his other children. But Joseph, like Cinderella, is turned into a slave, and, like her, he miraculously escapes and ends by surpassing his siblings. BRUNO BETTELHEIM

Bruno Bettelheim develops this paragraph in three ways: (1) He offers a *definition* of sibling rivalry by (2) explaining the *cause-and-effect* relationship between a parent's behavior toward one child and another child's anxiety over this behavior. (3) Bettelheim then cites two *examples* of sibling rivalry—one from the Bible (the story of Joseph) and one from fairy-tale literature (Cinderella). Notice how clearly the author announces his examples: "This is indicated in stories. . . ."

A CHECKLIST FOR WRITING PARAGRAPHS

You should find this list of questions helpful in evaluating the effectiveness of the paragraphs you write. The answer to each question should be *yes*.

1. Can you identify a topic sentence, either stated or unstated, that will function as a summary of the paragraph?
2. Can you explain your reasons for using a deductive (or inductive) organization in the paragraph?
3. Is the paragraph unified? Does the content of every sentence relate directly to the topic sentence?
4. Is the paragraph coherent? Does each sentence follow logically from the preceding sentence and lead logically to the next?
5. Have you used an easily recognizable method for arranging sentences in the paragraph—chronological, spatial, topical?
6. Have you used an easily recognized pattern for developing the content of the paragraph—e.g., example, comparison/contrast, etc.?

16

Arranging Groups of Paragraphs: Writing Business Letters, Memoranda, Reports, and Compositions for School

Whether you are composing business or personal letters, memoranda, reports, or compositions for school, most likely you'll need to write more than single paragraphs—in which case, you should be concerned with how the paragraphs are arranged.

The larger composition—in its arrangement and development of detail and in the function of its organizing sentence— is similar to the individual paragraph. When organizing a paragraph, the writer must think in terms of sentences and the logical progression from one sentence to the next. When organizing a letter or report, the writer must think in terms of *paragraphs* and the logical progression from one paragraph to the next. The likeness between individual paragraphs and larger groupings can be represented pictorially (see facing page).

In this diagram, the arrows extending from each of the sentences back to the topic sentence, and from each of the paragraphs back to the thesis statement, indicate that *unity* is a principle that applies to both the paragraph and the larger composition: in each form, component parts should be related to a single, organizing sentence. The arrows between sentences and between paragraphs indicate that both sentences within the paragraph and paragraphs within the larger composition should be clearly related to one another: the principle of *coherence* applies to each form.

In the sections that follow, you'll read about the considerations to bear in mind when organizing groups of paragraphs. These considerations range from broad concerns such as understanding your purpose in writing, and considering your audience, to specific concerns such as arranging and developing details to support a thesis and using specific techniques for introductions, transitions, and conclusions.

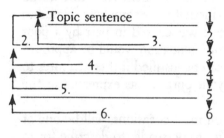

Paragraph

In a well-constructed paragraph, every sentence leads logically to the next and, at the same time, refers back to the topic sentence.

In a well-constructed composition, every paragraph leads logically to the next and, at the same time, refers back to the thesis statement.

Letters, Memoranda, Compositions

Introduction

Thesis Statement

Paragraph 2

Paragraph 3

Paragraph 4

Conclusion

PURPOSE

Before beginning a letter, report, or composition for school, it is essential that you understand your purpose in writing. Defining a purpose will allow you to focus your discussion quickly. If you know, for instance, that you are writing a report to evaluate the productivity of your work group, then you could outline the broad sections of that report before beginning. You would also know what information to include and exclude. Does your request for improved employee benefits belong in the report? Probably not, since your purpose is to evaluate productivity. But if you could demonstrate that low productivity was somehow related to low morale—and that low morale was caused in part by a poor benefits package, then your recommendation would be appropriate. Any discussion in an essay can be justified if it contributes to the reader's understanding of your purpose, as expressed in the thesis (see pages 231-4).

Your purpose in writing, on most occasions, will be one or more of the following: to inform, to persuade, to describe (or to achieve an objective closely associated with these). Description is discussed in some detail in Chapter 15 (see pages 220–23). Writing to persuade and to inform are discussed below.

Writing to Inform

When writing to inform, you give an account of an event, a person's behavior, an emotional state; justify an act; explain the process by which some mechanism or system works; or make comprehensible a puzzle or dilemma. When presenting information, you should do the following:

1. Clearly define your subject and any terms that might confuse a reader.
2. Divide your subject into component parts, each of which you can discuss in a paragraph or two; discuss each part thoroughly, and discuss each part in relation to the whole.

3. Provide examples to clarify generalizations.
4. Possess the experience to speak knowledgeably on the subject (or refer to sources who are knowledgeable).

Some information is so easily explained that following these steps is unnecessary. For more complex informative presentations, however, these recommendations should be useful.

Writing to Persuade

When writing to persuade, your purpose is to influence the thinking of a reader. To accomplish this goal, you can appeal to the reader's reason or to his emotion. If your appeal is to reason, then the evidence you use should both support and differ from your conclusions. By presenting only material that supports your conclusions, you may be accused of "stacking the evidence" in your favor. Be fair-minded in summarizing any evidence contrary to your views. You should also try to assure that your reasoning proceeds logically. For example, it is illogical to suggest that because one event precedes another in time, the second event has been caused by the first. (If a stork flew over your house two hours before you were born, is it logical to conclude that the stork had anything to do with your birth?) It would also be illogical to argue against an idea by attacking the character of the person who holds it. Appeals to logic should be based on the merits of a presentation.

The following is a standard method for arranging an *appeal to logic:*

1. Introduce your topic and state your position.
2. Consider the evidence that supports your view.
3. Consider the evidence contrary to your view.
4. Compare and contrast the evidence.
5. Conclude in favor of your view. (Alternately, you could accept a portion of your opponent's position and, in the conclusion, modify your view.)

You might also attempt to persuade your reader by appealing to his or her emotions. You could make an emotional appeal to the reader's desire for self-preservation, self-esteem, personal gain, or personal pleasure. You might arrange an *emotional appeal* as follows:

1. Introduce your idea.
2. Explain why accepting this idea will help your reader to
   * feel more secure (self-preservation);
   * feel better about himself (self-esteem);
   * increase his leisure time (personal pleasure).
3. Conclude by reasoning that these benefits merit the reader's accepting your idea.

AUDIENCE

With each new writing task, determine the person who will be reading your memorandum, letter, etc., and direct the tone and the level of complexity of your writing to him or her. Discover what your readers know about your subject. The more knowledgeable they are, the less you should review fundamentals and supply background information. At the same time, readers who have no specialized knowledge of your subject will be confused if you assume they are familiar with technical or professional terms, or with the history of a particular issue.

For example, assume that you are writing a memorandum to suggest that your company purchase a computer, and you want to convince both the office staff, which generally has no training in computers, and your employer, who receives specialized magazines on office automation. It would make sense to send two memoranda, one tailored to the needs of each audience. You might appeal to the staff by describing computer applications that would relieve drudgery; at the same time, you might want to allay the staff's fears of being replaced by machines. You would appeal on more technical terms to your employer and argue that increased efficiency and accuracy warrant the purchase. Ultimately, the two memoranda have the same purpose; but your methods for achieving this purpose would vary depending on an assessment of the needs of each audience.

You should also be sensitive to the tone that your readers expect from a piece of writing. Many people dislike the use of slang expressions for formal occasions (such as business correspondence, reports, and compositions for the classroom). For instance, some might object to the following:

> We offered the proposal, and Mr. Larkin ate it up.

A formal version of the same sentence reads as follows:

> We offered the proposal, and Mr. Larkin accepted it without qualification.

An inappropriately chosen tone or level of complexity that offends or intimidates will quickly call (negative) attention to itself. The converse is not true, however: if your tone and level of complexity are appropriate to your writing task, then the reader most likely will not notice—concentrating, instead, on the message you wish to communicate.

THESIS STATEMENTS

The function of a thesis statement is to focus and organize the content of a letter, memorandum, or composition—each of which comprises a series of paragraphs. A thesis statement, in many respects, has the same function as the topic sentence of a paragraph. Both are used as a basis for including information in a discussion or excluding it; both help readers to anticipate the organization of the sentences or paragraphs that follow. Because the functions of the thesis statement and the topic sentence are parallel, a quick review of pages 202–4, on writing topic sentences, should be useful as an introduction to this section.

A thesis statement, like any other sentence, contains a subject and a predicate. What distinguishes the thesis from other sentences, including topic sentences, is its level of generality: the thesis is more general, allowing for a discussion that is developed over a number of paragraphs. The length of this discussion—whether one page or one hundred pages—will depend on the subject you choose and the claim you make about it. In most cases, the more general the subject and the more complex the predicate, the longer your discussion will be. You must therefore take care in writing thesis statements, seeking a balance between the general and the specific that will allow you to discuss your ideas at a length appropriate to your writing task. Choosing a thesis statement involves these two steps:

STEP 1: DISTINGUISH YOUR TOPIC FROM YOUR SUBJECT.

A subject is a broad area of concern that can be divided into more specific topics. "Automobiles," for example, is a broad subject comprising the topics *autos for work, autos for recreation, autos for status, autos for economy,* and so on. When writing a letter, memorandum, or report, you will typically begin with a subject, an idea too large and still too vague in conception to be discussed thoroughly in a reasonable amount of space. (If you begin with a narrowly focused topic, all the better.) Attempting to write a brief report on automobiles would be futile if you wished to provide detailed information. You would need to narrow the subject—perhaps to *autos for economy*. If your employer asked for a report in which you recommend an economical car, would you be able to do so? Probably. But you would have a much easier time if you narrowed your subject still further, by determining the price that the company could afford; whether the company needed a station wagon, van, truck, passenger car; and so on. You could narrow the subject as follows:

SUBJECT   automobiles
LIMITED SUBJECT automobiles for economy
TOPIC   station wagons costing $7500

The subject has now been narrowed to a topic appropriate for a detailed, relatively brief treatment.

STEP 2: DETERMINE THE PURPOSE OF YOUR LETTER, REPORT, OR
ESSAY, AND CHOOSE A PREDICATE THAT REFLECTS THIS PURPOSE.
A thesis statement—and thereby the structure of a composition—depends entirely on your purpose in writing. If you are
writing to inform or describe, let the reader know this in the
predicate of your thesis. Imply, if not state directly, that you will
use one (but probably more) of the following methods of developing your topic: summary, comparison, contrast, definition, illus-
tration, application of one concept to another, description, and
interpretation. When organized in this way, a thesis will give you
direction for planning and your reader direction for anticipating
the rest of the composition. In terms of our example, you might
write the following:

> Important considerations to bear in mind when comparing station
> wagons that cost $7500 are mechanical reliability, fuel economy,
> and passenger comfort.

In this example, notice how the topic has been limited so that you
could discuss it thoroughly in a few pages. The claim made about
the topic—that important considerations for comparison are mechanical reliability, fuel economy, and passenger comfort—would
allow you to plan and the reader to expect a comparison and
contrast. Having decided to use three criteria, you could structure
the remainder of the composition in a straightforward manner—
devoting one or two paragraphs to each criterion and a concluding
paragraph to a summary of your findings.

If your purpose in writing is to persuade, then you should
assert in the predicate of your thesis statement a definite opinion
about your topic—a claim with which readers can either agree or
disagree. After making this claim, you should support it with
convincing arguments. The thesis of a composition or report
intended to inform can easily be changed into a thesis intended
to persuade:

> Having compared the mechanical reliability, fuel economy, and
> passenger comfort of several station wagons costing $7500, I
> would recommend ———.

Notice that the topic of this argumentative thesis remains sub-
stantially the same as the topic of the informational thesis. What
changes is the predicate. Here, you're stating that you'll not only
review information about the station wagons with respect to three
criteria, but will also assert a definite opinion: "I recommend
_____." This thesis statement would allow you to structure your
letter or report in a straightforward manner, devoting one or two
paragraphs to a discussion of each criterion and a final two or
three paragraphs to a specific recommendation.

Though these sample thesis statements have been limited to
station wagons, the general principles that have been discussed
apply to all thesis statements. *To summarize, the effective thesis
possesses these qualities:*

- The topic's level of generality is appropriate to the writing task.
- The claim made about the topic in the predicate reflects the
  purpose of the report, essay, etc.—that is, to inform, to persuade, to recommend, and so on.
- The claim made in the predicate is appropriately complex.

(**Note:** by their nature, personal letters are informal and do not
require such carefully structured elements as a thesis statement.)

It is common for writers to begin with a thesis and, in the
process of writing, discover that the thesis changes. When this
occurs, start another draft of your work, organizing it around the
new thesis. It is also common to have in mind a general subject
but no firm topic about which to write. If this happens, in order
to generate ideas try brainstorming—making lists, writing for
fifteen minutes without interruption, letting your mind wander
over the various aspects of your subject. Then examine what
you've written. At this point, you'll probably be able to extract
some ideas for a topic that you can then fashion into a thesis.

The discussions of paragraph unity, coherence, arrangement, and development found in Chapter 15 apply to the larger forms of writing: the letter, the report, and the composition. For the sake of brevity, material that can be found in that chapter will not be repeated in the sections that follow.

ARRANGEMENT OF PARAGRAPHS

Once you have decided on a thesis statement (whether it is preliminary or final), you need to determine which aspects of the topic to include in the various sections of your composition. The overall arrangement of your work will probably be inductive or deductive, as was the case with individual paragraphs. That is, you'll begin with details and lead to a general point—your thesis; or you'll begin with a thesis and support it with details. Plan out the relationship among sections of the composition. How will the supporting details you've selected for one paragraph lead to the next paragraph? As with individual paragraphs, groups of paragraphs can be arranged spatially, chronologically, or topically (see pages 211–13).

For instance, a memorandum written to summarize the events of a week-long business conference might be divided into seven paragraphs: one paragraph for the introduction; one paragraph for each day's proceedings (five paragraphs total); and one paragraph for the conclusion. The body of the memorandum would be arranged chronologically—Monday, Tuesday, etc. Any combination of techniques for the arrangement of paragraphs within a letter or report is acceptable, provided your presentation is systematic and readily accessible to the reader.

DEVELOPMENT

Once you have determined which aspects of the topic you will pursue in support of your thesis, as well as the approximate location of each aspect within the larger structure of the letter or report, you can turn your attention to development. As you read in Chapter 15, paragraphs are developed according to patterns of definition, process, example, comparison/contrast, cause/effect, and description. (See pages 213–23.) Combining these techniques is commonplace. For instance, a letter detailing the reasons a customer should buy your exercise machine and not the competition's might be developed as follows:

Introductory paragraph	State what you would like your reader to do.
Paragraph 2	Define the qualities of a good exercise machine.
Paragraph 3	Cite your product as an example.
Paragraph 4	Cite your competitor's product as another example.
Paragraph 5	Compare and contrast the two products.
Concluding paragraph	Summarize your discussion.

Every letter, memorandum, or composition presents a different challenge for developing your material. Keep in mind that any combination of developmental techniques is acceptable as long as the end result—your letter, report, etc.—meets the tests of unity and coherence.

UNITY

A letter, memorandum, or composition for school is said to be unified if the topic sentence of each paragraph refers directly to the thesis statement. (See discussion of unity in paragraphs, pages 206–7.)

COHERENCE

A letter, memorandum, or composition for school is said to be coherent if each paragraph follows logically from the preceding paragraph and leads logically to the next. (See discussion of coherence in paragraphs, pages 207–8.)

GROUPS OF PARAGRAPHS IN CONTEXT

A brief, five-paragraph article provides an opportunity to apply the terminology discussed thus far. Though this article appeared in a national magazine, it is similar in structure to brief essays assigned by high-school or college teachers. Examples of business correspondence and memoranda will follow later in this chapter.

THE FUTURE OF THE INCOME HANG-UP

Contemporary couples may be too bound by traditional 1 roles and too set in their ways to accept wives of equal, not to mention greater, job status. Will today's young people—the married couples of the 1990s—be any less rigid? Probably not.

Jane Daniels, director of the Women in Engineering Pro- 2 gram at Purdue University, has been counseling first-year female students there for 10 years, and observes that the students' main source of anxiety hasn't changed. "In every seminar I've taught, including this year's," Daniels says, "the girls are worried about having a career in engineering because they are afraid of earning more than their future husbands—or of just having a more prestigious job."

Anxiety about nontraditional economic roles may still be 3 prevalent among teenagers, but most now say that they believe that wives should earn money and that husbands should help with domestic chores. In 1980, researchers Regula Herzog and Jerald Bachman of the University of Michigan surveyed a randomly selected group of 3,000 high-school seniors and found that only 13 percent of the boys desired a nonworking wife—and only 4 percent of the girls wanted to be one. Indeed, 92 percent of the girls expected to have a career—other than homemaker—by age 30. Both boys and girls said that couples should share equally in child care and housework.

But as soon as they imagined having their own children, the students abandoned their progressive views. When a couple has preschool children, most said, the wife should stay at home. Well over half rejected the idea that the husband do more than an equal share of housework, and both boys and girls were overwhelmingly opposed to an arrangement in which the husband worked less than the wife.

The researchers found that the husband of the future, very much like the husband of the present, "is the one likely to be held accountable and to feel the greatest psychological burden, if economic support for the family is not adequate." Like their elders, then, the younger generation believes that real men don't earn less than their wives. Should some of them eventually become part of a couple in which the wife outperforms her husband, they, like their counterparts today, may find themselves in rough marital waters.   CARIN RUBENSTEIN

Reprinted from *Psychology Today Magazine.*
Copyright © 1982 American Psychological Association.

ANALYSIS

PURPOSE:

Rubenstein's purpose is persuasive. She presents information designed to appeal to our reason, and on the basis of this information reaches her conclusion, which is stated in the final paragraph and in the thesis.

AUDIENCE:

Rubenstein uses the evidence of university researchers to persuade her readers. From this, one can infer that she writes for an educated audience that expects documentation for her broad claims.

THESIS STATEMENT:
Rubenstein's first paragraph serves as her thesis.

ARRANGEMENT:
The essay is organized deductively, with Rubenstein's thesis coming first, followed by topically arranged details. In paragraph 2, Rubenstein establishes that teenagers are anxious about women holding prestigious jobs, a finding that directly supports her thesis. In paragraph 3, she cites research describing teenagers' attitudes about the role of childless women and men in the work force. Paragraph 4 is devoted to the change in these attitudes once children are born into a relationship in which both husband and wife work. The concluding paragraph is based on evidence presented in the previous paragraphs.

DEVELOPMENT:
Rubenstein carefully develops her material. In paragraph 2, she provides an example of the students' anxiety that is suggested in the first paragraph. Paragraphs 3 and 4 are devoted to a comparison and contrast of teenagers' attitudes about working couples who have or who don't have children. The discrepancy that emerges leads Rubenstein to her conclusion—in which she presents the conclusions of researchers and then speculates on possible marital tensions in the future.

UNITY:
The content of each of Rubenstein's paragraphs refers to the thesis and the ideas of rigidity and anxiety.

COHERENCE:
The relationship among Rubenstein's paragraphs is clear (for the reasons established in the discussions of arrangement and development).

Many writers attend to introductions, transitions, and conclusions only after they have written the body of their letter, report, or composition. The rationale for this delay is that these three elements can improve the quality of a composition only if it is *already* unified, coherent, and well-developed. Transitions are impossible to make if there is no clear logical relationship among paragraphs. And introductions and conclusions have little point if the composition is not focused.

INTRODUCTIONS

The purpose of an introduction is to familiarize readers with a topic before you offer a detailed discussion. Does your reader lack the background information necessary to appreciate your material? Do you need to stir the reader's interest? Are there preparations to make—a groundwork to lay, so to speak—before you can offer and then develop your ideas? If your answer to any of these is *yes,* then a carefully executed introduction is called for, one that will prepare the reader for the discussion that follows in the body of your letter, report, etc.

Context, purpose, and audience are the primary considerations to bear in mind when planning an introduction. Consider a few of the possible contexts: you could be writing for business, a letter to someone outside the company, an internal memorandum, or a report to a co-worker. You could be writing a term paper or a book report for an instructor or a newspaper or magazine article for a wider audience. The purpose of your writing could be to inform, persuade, describe, inquire, congratulate, complain, or recommend. You might know your readers well, only casually, or not at all—and your readers may know a great deal, or only a little, about your topic. The tone and the content of your introductions will vary, depending on the needs of the piece you are writing, the context in which you are writing, your familiarity with the readers, and the readers' familiarity with your subject.

Introductions to Business Letters and Memoranda

Business correspondence usually begins directly, with limited space devoted to introductions. If you are on friendly terms with your reader, you may want to begin with a brief, informal remark having nothing to do with the content of the letter:

Dear ———:
   After struggling for hours in waist-high snow drifts, I finally made it into the office. It seems that spring will never come to Albany, and I don't know if my back can take much more shoveling.
   You'll remember that at our last meeting . . .

If you do not know your reader—and especially if he or she is positioned several rungs above you on the corporate ladder—you'll want to use a direct, formal approach:

Dear ———:
   I am writing in response to your request that . . .
      OR
   I am writing to request that . . .
      OR
   I am writing to call your attention to . . .
      OR
   In response to your letter of . . .

Memoranda circulated within a company, and letters written to complain, congratulate, recommend, or inquire most often begin directly, with no introduction.

Introductions to Essays and Reports

The essay is a specialized form of writing found in few places other than classrooms and magazines. In an essay, the writer's job is to offer and then reflect upon a topic, at times supplying information, at times speculating, at times arguing. The purpose of any introduction is to engage the reader's interest, but this is especially important for the essay, which people read on a more voluntary basis than a business report. The introduction to essays as well as to reports should be calculated to stimulate the readers' interests, to make them *want* to read on.

The writer may try to engage a reader by starting with an anecdote, a poignant story to illustrate some central concern raised later in the body of the essay. In another case the writer may begin with an evocative quotation:

> "My home town is so dull," goes the old gag, "that for excitement everybody goes down to McDonald's to watch the numbers on the sign change." McDonald's in recent years has been selling hamburgers so fast (140 per sec.) that many golden-arched signs state simply: BILLIONS AND BILLIONS SOLD. But that does not mean that McDonald's has lost count. Indeed, the Illinois-based company (1983 sales: $3.1 billion) disclosed last week that it will sell its 50 billionth hamburger some time late this month or in early November [1984]. The tally goes back to 1948, when hamburger No. 1 went on the grill at the McDonald brothers' drive-in restaurant in San Bernardino, Calif. McDonald's acknowledges that it will be unable to single out the 50 billionth patty among its restaurants in 31 countries. But it says that its computer analysts will be able to estimate roughly, about ten days ahead of time, the day and the hour the historic burger will be served. At that time, the company will stage a numbers-popping celebration with prizes for customers.

Reports for business and the classroom are intended to inform and/or persuade. These types of writing often require the reader to be familiar with background information before the actual discussion begins. In such cases, a brief historical review, an analysis of a problem, or the review of a controversy can function well as an introduction. Two examples follow:

BRIEF HISTORICAL REVIEW

> Twenty years ago, Congress passed the first laws against sex discrimination in the workplace. Ten years ago, a flurry of multi-million-dollar lawsuits—some brought by women, others by the government—sent corporations scrambling to comply with the regulations on equal opportunity and affirmative action for women. How much has changed since then? Are the changes

cosmetic, or are they deep and permanent? To answer these questions, I conducted a cross-country survey of American companies. I found each corporation unique, yet certain trends seem clear. . . . CLAIRE SAFRAN

Notice the chronological arrangement of information in this introduction: proceeding from twenty years ago—when laws were passed against sexual discrimination in the workplace—to the present, in which questions regarding current reactions are raised.

REVIEW OF A CONTROVERSY

Censorship is a problem that cuts to the heart of American democracy. Many argue forcefully that the rights of a community take priority over the rights of individuals—that, for instance, because pornography is sordid and can psychologically scar the innocent, no individual should have the right to produce and distribute it. There are those who take the opposite view, that what makes this country unique is its constitutional guarantee of individual liberties—including the liberty to produce and to read material that some might find offensive. The argument for censorship is controversial because proponents want to legislate morality; the argument against censorship is equally controversial because proponents are placed in the position of defending, out of principle, practices which they may detest. Between these apparently irreconcilable views there must lie a responsible middle ground, one which protects the rights of both the community and the individual. Over the years, four distinct compromises have been offered to achieve such a middle ground, but only one seems workable today.

The first compromise. . . .

This paragraph is an introduction to a term paper on censorship in America, written for a class in history. Notice how the writer reviews the opposing views on the issue, stating each view and the reason it is controversial.

The length of an introduction depends entirely on the length and complexity of your writing task—longer introductions, of one or more pages, being most appropriate for complex discussions. Let a sense of proportion be your guide: an introduction should never overwhelm the body of your report or essay.

TRANSITIONS

A transition is any expression that eases a reader's passage from one idea or mood to another. A writer will use transitions within and between paragraphs to refer a reader back to what he has just read and forward to what is still to come. Effective transitions always serve this double function, helping the writer to provide "bridges," so to speak, between stages of his thought. The more bridges that are provided, the easier the reader can move from one idea to the next.

Here is a list of some of the most commonly used transitions:

although	either/or	since
and	for	so
another	however	still another
because	just as/so too	therefore
before	nor	thus
but	not only/but also	while
consequently	or	

See also pages 28–35 for more discussion on the use of transitions.

CONCLUSIONS

In a conclusion, you should restate, briefly but precisely, the main ideas of your letter, memorandum, report, or composition. In addition to this brief summary, you may also want to discuss the *significance* of your ideas. What are their implications—to what new questions do they lead? How can they shed light on other concerns? The conclusion should crystallize your purpose in writing and your audience's purpose in reading what you've written.

If much of what you write is routine business correspondence, you should not make dramatic flourishes in your conclusions—these would only upset the balance of your letter or memo.

End business letters with short, crisp conclusions—just a few sentences long:

> These recommendations should meet your company's needs. If you would like to discuss particular points in detail, please don't hesitate to call. Thank you for your careful consideration.
>
> Very truly y~urs,

The following expressions are commonly found in the concluding sentences of letters, memos, reports, and compositions.

as you can see	to summarize	in summary
in review	therefore	thus
the point, then, is that . . .	in conclusion	finally
it should be clear that . . .		

The principles discussed in this chapter for writing effective compositions apply to a wide variety of contexts—from business letters to essays for school, to letters of inquiry and complaint, to detailed reports. Having completed a composition, you should be satisfied that your purpose is clearly stated; your tone and level of complexity are appropriate for the reader's needs; your thesis statement is sufficiently specific and that each paragraph's topic sentence refers to it; your paragraphs are logically arranged and carefully developed; and your introductions, transitions, and conclusions aid the reader's understanding.

Attention to these larger elements of a composition, combined with attention to grammatical writing and acceptable usage, should lead to successful communication—which, above all, is your purpose. If you cannot express ideas clearly, regardless of what you perceive to be their worth, they will go unappreciated. Without question, *what* you say is intimately bound up with *how* you say it. This is why grammatical, well-organized writing makes a difference.

FORMATS FOR BUSINESS LETTERS AND MEMORANDA

Now that you are familiar with the principles of writing effective compositions, consider a particular application: the writing of business letters and memoranda.

Qualities of Effective Letters

Here are six suggestions for writing letters that exhibit a clarity of purpose and a self-confident, though not overconfident, tone:

1. Talk *to* your reader, not *at* him: imagine yourself seated in the same room, speaking your letter.

   • Be natural. Avoid stilted business*ese* (expressions like "herewith, as per, kindly confirm same, esteemed favor").
   • Be tactful. Avoid accusations or demands. Of course, there is a time to be firm, such as in letters of complaint. But there is an offensive and less offensive way of saying anything.

   NOT   You were wrong to say . . .
   BUT   My information differs from yours. . . .

   NOT   You said that you were going to . . .
   BUT   You'll remember that you offered to . . .

2. Have a definite purpose for writing: Express the *who, what, where, when,* and *why* of the letter in the first sentence—or the second sentence if you begin with an informal, personal greeting.

3. Be sure that your information is accurate and that your presentation is well structured. (See Chapter 15 and pages 226–7 of this chapter.)

4. Be sure that your presentation is grammatical.

5. Be precise. If you are writing *an order* or *a letter of inquiry,* describe exactly the needed information or product, including

all pertinent catalogue or order numbers. (If you are not ordering from a catalogue or an advertisement, mention where you first saw or heard about the product. This will help your correspondent identify the item in question.)

- If you are writing *a letter of complaint,* adopt a tone that will achieve results. Do not insult your reader.
- If you are *following up on a letter or phone conversation,* summarize for your reader the current state of affairs between you. (Mention dates of previous correspondence, if necessary.) Then write the body of your letter.

6. Avoid messy erasures and white-outs. The appearance of your letter is important.

Standard Information

There are various formats for writing business letters, two of which follow. (See example letters, pages 252–3.) Regardless of the format you choose, your letter will contain five elements:

1. **The return address** contains your street address; city, state, and zip code; and the date. Do not use abbreviations. Note: On letterhead stationery, only the date needs to be supplied. It should be centered one or two lines below the last line of the letterhead.

2. **The inside address** contains the name and title of the person to whom you are writing; his/her company; the company's suite or room number (if any); the street address; and the city, state, and zip code. Use no abbreviations unless the company does so on its own stationery.

   Note: Brief titles are separated from a name by a comma. Longer titles take two lines.

   Mrs. Elisha Phillips, President

   Mrs. Jane Logan, Director
   Budget and Management Division

   Mrs. Susan Crane
   Assistant to the President

3. **The salutation** offers your greetings to the reader of the letter. Place a colon after the salutation:

   Dear Mr. ———:

   Dear Mrs./Miss/Ms. ———: (If you do not know a woman's marital status, use Ms.)

   Sirs:

   Madam:

   Gentlemen: (Use these salutations when you are not writing to

   To whom it may concern: a particular person.)

   Sir or Madam:

   Note: Avoid duplicating titles.

   NOT   Dr. Rachel Adams, M.D.

   BUT   Rachel Adams, M.D. *or* Dr. Rachel Adams

   If you are not writing to a particular person within a company, write an *attention line* two lines below the inside address and two lines above the salutation:

   Alban Electronics
   231 Allspice Drive
   Armonk, New York 12215

   Attention: Marketing Department

   Sir or Madam:

4. **The body** of the letter, divided into well-developed paragraphs, expresses your letter's content.

5. **The closing** consists of some complimentary remark (such as *Yours truly, Sincerely*), your signature, and your typed name and position (below your signature). Note: only the first letter of a closing remark is capitalized, and the last word is followed by a comma (*e.g.*, Very truly yours,).

Abbreviated Matter

Standard abbreviations, placed at the left-hand margin of a letter (two lines below the closing) have a specific meaning in business correspondence:

```
                              Very truly yours,

                              Joshua Franks

                              Joshua Franks, Director
                              Advertising Department

      JF/dm
      Enc.
      cc:  Mr. Alex Brand
           Ms. Sarah Gerard
```

When a secretary or typist has typed a letter, the initials (in capital letters) of the person who has signed the letter are followed by a slash and the lower-case initials of the secretary or typist. Skip two lines after the closing and place the initials at the left-hand margin.

Placed on the line following the initials, at the left-hand margin, is the word *Enclosure* or the abbreviation *Enc.*, if material other than the letter is included in the envelope.

Inform the reader that carbon copies or photocopies of a letter have been sent to others by placing *cc:* and the names of the people who have received copies on the line below *Enc.*

Spacing

All business letters should be typewritten, and all—with the exception of very short ones—should be single-spaced.

The choice between block (see p. 252) and semiblock (see p. 253) format is a matter of personal preference. Each is considered correct; block is, perhaps, the more formal. If you use a block format, do not indent the first word of each paragraph; if you use a semiblock format, indent the first word of each paragraph five spaces. Indent the paragraphs of short, double-spaced letters.

Skip a line between single-spaced paragraphs.

Set off quoted matter or lists longer than three lines as follows:

• If no indentation is used in regular paragraphing, indent five spaces from the left margin.

• If indentation *is* used in regular paragraphing, indent ten spaces from the left margin.

A Business Letter's Second Page

Do not use a second page if only the closing of the letter remains to be typed. Fit the closing on the first page or restructure the letter.

Do not leave a paragraph of only two lines at the bottom of the first page of a letter; do not begin the second page with fewer than three lines of a paragraph.

Do not use letterhead stationery for the second page of a letter. Use a blank, unlined sheet of typing paper, the same weight as the first page.

Type a heading on the second page of a letter to prevent confusion in case the first and second pages are separated. The heading should include the name of the person to whom you are writing, the date, and the page number.

```
Mr. Norman Lubber
November 8, 1985
Page 2


Depending on the number of participants, the seminar takes

four to six days.  Half-day follow-up sessions . . .
```

Envelopes

Use a block format (see below); single-space the address.

Center the address between the right- and left-hand edges and slightly below center vertically.

If you are not using letterhead stationery, place your return address at the upper left corner of the envelope.

If you are not writing to a particular person within a company, write an *attention line* two or three lines below the address at the left-hand margin of the envelope.

If the letter is *confidential* and addressed to a particular person, type *confidential* in capitals and underline it. Place the remark two or three lines below the address at the left-hand margin of the envelope.

```
11 Park Street
Suite 602
Washington, D.C. 20016




                    Wyoming Outfitters
                    84 Tremont Street
                    Lander, Wyoming  82520


Attention:  Marketing Department
```

Block Format

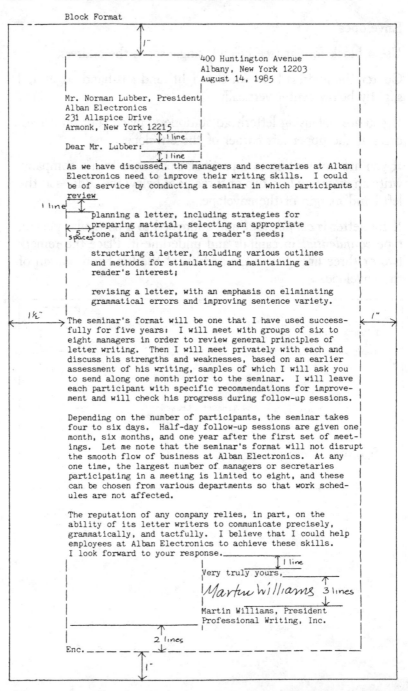

400 Huntington Avenue
Albany, New York 12203
August 14, 1985

Mr. Norman Lubber, President
Alban Electronics
231 Allspice Drive
Armonk, New York 12215

Dear Mr. Lubber:

As we have discussed, the managers and secretaries at Alban
Electronics need to improve their writing skills. I could
be of service by conducting a seminar in which participants
review

    planning a letter, including strategies for
    preparing material, selecting an appropriate
    tone, and anticipating a reader's needs;

    structuring a letter, including various outlines
    and methods for stimulating and maintaining a
    reader's interest;

    revising a letter, with an emphasis on eliminating
    grammatical errors and improving sentence variety.

The seminar's format will be one that I have used successfully for five years: I will meet with groups of six to
eight managers in order to review general principles of
letter writing. Then I will meet privately with each and
discuss his strengths and weaknesses, based on an earlier
assessment of his writing, samples of which I will ask you
to send along one month prior to the seminar. I will leave
each participant with specific recommendations for improvement and will check his progress during follow-up sessions.

Depending on the number of participants, the seminar takes
four to six days. Half-day follow-up sessions are given one
month, six months, and one year after the first set of meetings. Let me note that the seminar's format will not disrupt
the smooth flow of business at Alban Electronics. At any
one time, the largest number of managers or secretaries
participating in a meeting is limited to eight, and these
can be chosen from various departments so that work schedules are not affected.

The reputation of any company relies, in part, on the
ability of its letter writers to communicate precisely,
grammatically, and tactfully. I believe that I could help
employees at Alban Electronics to achieve these skills.
I look forward to your response.

Very truly yours,

Martin Williams

Martin Williams, President
Professional Writing, Inc.

Enc.

Semiblock Format

Return Address ⎱ 400 Huntington Avenue
Albany, New York 12203
August 14, 1985

Mr. Norman Lubber, President ⎱
Alban Electronics
231 Allspice Drive   — Inside Address
Armonk, New York 12215

Dear Mr. Lubber: ⎱ Salutation

5 spaces
As we have discussed, the managers and secretaries
at Alban Electronics need to improve their writing skills.
I could be of service by conducting a seminar in which
participants review

planning a letter, including strategies
for preparing material, selecting an
appropriate tone, and anticipating a
reader's needs;

10 spaces
structuring a letter, including various
outlines and methods for stimulating and
maintaining a reader's interest;

revising a letter, with an emphasis on
eliminating grammatical errors and
improving sentence variety.

Body ⎱
The seminar's format will be one that I have used
successfully for five years: I will meet with groups of six
to eight managers in order to review general principles of
letter writing. Then I will meet privately with each and
discuss his strengths and weaknesses, based on an earlier
assessment of his writing, samples of which I will ask you
to send along one month prior to the seminar. I will leave
each participant with specific recommendations for improvement and will check his progress during follow-up sessions.

Depending on the number of participants, the seminar
takes four to six days. Half-day follow-up sessions are
given one month, six months, and one year after the first set
of meetings. Let me note that the seminar's format will not
disrupt the smooth flow of business at Alban Electronics.
At any one time, the largest number of managers or secretaries
participating in a meeting is limited to eight, and these
can be chosen from various departments so that work schedules
are not affected.

The reputation of any company relies, in part, on the
ability of its letter writers to communicate precisely,
grammatically, and tactfully. I believe that I could help
employees at Alban Electronics to achieve these skills.
I look forward to your response.

Very truly yours,

Closing and Signature ⎱ Martin Williams

Martin Williams, President
Professional Writing, Inc.

Enc.

```
                              MEMO


DATE:   May 24, 1985

TO:  Mike Frank, Accounting Department

FROM:  Hank Peters (HP)

RE:  IRS audit

        Please stop by my office on 6/10/85 at 10 a.m. and
        review with me the presentation you will make to the IRS
        officer in July.  I am asking Mary Atkins to attend both
        our meeting and the audit itself.

        Please bring with you all pertinent documents.  Call
        Howard Dawes (ext. 290) if you need help carrying
        printouts, etc.

                        H.P.


HP/ws
cc:  Mary Atkins
```

A Format for Memoranda

A memorandum is an interoffice document designed to request or to provide information or an opinion. The memorandum's format shares a few characteristics with the business letter:

Note the positioning of the left-hand margin for the body of the memorandum.

Use single spacing, with two spaces between paragraphs. Do not indent paragraphs in a brief memorandum.

Use abbreviated matter as you would in a standard business letter. (See page 249.)

Note that the return and inside addresses, as well as the closing, are absent from a memorandum. Typed initials are acceptable as a closing. Signed initials should follow the FROM line in the heading if you have not typed the memorandum.

Sources

The author wishes to acknowledge the sources of the quotations that appear in this volume.

CHAPTER 1
Stephen Crane, "The Bride Comes to Yellow Sky," in Nancy Sullivan, ed., *The Treasury of American Short Stories* (Garden City, N.Y.: Doubleday, 1981), p. 193.
Erich Fromm, *Escape from Freedom* (New York: Rinehart, 1941), p. 29.
Raymond Chandler, *The Big Sleep* (New York: Vintage Books, 1976), p. 1.
H. Arthur Klein, *Surfing* (Philadelphia: Lippincott, 1965), p. 49.
Robert Jastrow, "Toward an Intelligence Beyond Man's," *Time*, February 20, 1978.
Gore Vidal in interview with Dick Cavett, in Norman Mailer's *Pieces and Pontifications* (Boston: Little, Brown, 1982), p. 63.
Carl Goeller, *Writing and Selling Greeting Cards* (Boston: The Writer, 1981), p. 3.
John R. Erickson, *The Modern Cowboy* (Lincoln: University of Nebraska Press, 1982), p. 11.
Katherine Davis Fishman, *The Computer Establishment* (New York: McGraw-Hill, 1982), p. 77.
Arthur C. Clarke, "Electronic Tutors," *Omni*, June 1980, p. 77.
John Steinbeck, *Travels with Charley in Search of America* (New York: Viking, 1962), p. 3.

CHAPTER 2

Stanley Jay Shapiro, *Exploring Environmental Careers* (New York: Richard Rosen Press, 1982), p. 5.

Martha Ture, "The West Coast Girds for the Gypsy Moth," *Sierra,* 68, No. 3 (May/June 1983), p. 26.

Susan West, *Science 84,* No. 5 (Jan./Feb.), p. 1.

Sharon Whitney, *Eleanor Roosevelt* (New York: Franklin Watts, 1982), p. 4.

CHAPTER 3

Harold Holzer, "Mark Twain Returns to Hannibal," *American History,* 18, No. 3 (May 1983), pp. 26–33.

Henry David Thoreau, *Walden: Or Life in the Woods* (New York: Signet, 1960), p. 65.

Carl C. Taylor et al., *Rural Life in the United States* (New York: Alfred A. Knopf, 1949), p. 12.

William J. Baker, *Sports in the Western World* (Totowa, N.J.: Rowman and Littlefield, c1982), p. 1.

CHAPTER 4

Annie Dillard, "The Death of the Moth," in J. M. Wasson, *Subject and Structure,* 6th Ed. (Boston: Little, Brown, 1978).

CHAPTER 5

Frances Mossiker, *Napoleon and Josephine: The Biography of a Marriage* (New York: Simon & Schuster, 1964), pp. 16–22.

CHAPTER 6

Lois Decker O'Neil, ed., *The Woman's Book of World Records and Achievements* (Garden City, N.Y.: Doubleday, 1979), p. 690.

George Sullivan, *Better Field Events for Girls* (New York: Dodd, Mead, 1982), p. 14.

Ronald Jessup, *The Wonderful World of Archaeology* (Garden City, N.Y.: Doubleday, 1968), p. 25.

CHAPTER 10

Harrison E. Salisbury, *A Journey for Our Times: A Memoir* (New York: Harper & Row, 1983), p. 66.

William C. Ketchum, Jr., *Chests, Cupboards, Desks and Other Pieces* (New York: Alfred A. Knopf, 1982), p. 90.

Henry David Thoreau, "On the Duty of Civil Disobedience," *Walden and On the Duty of Civil Disobedience* (New York: The New American Library, 1960), pp. 222–25.

Arthur C. Clarke, "We'll Never Conquer Space," *Popular Mechanics,* 1960. Quotation from J. M. Wasson, *Subject and Structure,* 6th Ed. (Boston: Little, Brown, 1978), p. 491.

J. Bronowski, *The Ascent of Man* (Boston: Little, Brown, 1973), p. 427.

Joyce Carol Oates, "Bloodstains." Quotation from J. M. Wasson, *Subject and Structure,* 6th Ed. (Boston: Little, Brown, 1978), p. 279.

Katherine Davis Fishman, *The Computer Establishment* (New York: McGraw-Hill, 1982), p. 77.

Theodore Dreiser, "The Lost Phoebe," in Nancy Sullivan, ed., *The Treasury of American Short Stories* (Garden City, N.Y.: Doubleday, 1981), p. 204.

Mark Twain, "The £ 1,000,000 Bank-Note," in Nancy Sullivan, ed., *The Treasury of American Short Stories* (Garden City, N.Y.: Doubleday, 1981), p. 100.

Carl Sagan, *The Dragons of Eden: Speculations on the Evolution of Human Intelligence* (New York: Random House, 1977), p. 138.

Henry James, "The Real Thing," in Nancy Sullivan, ed., *The Treasury of American Short Stories* (Garden City, N.Y.: Doubleday, 1981), p. 132.

Leo Tolstoy, *Anna Karenina,* trans. Louise and Aylmer Maude (New York: Norton, 1970), p. 139.

S. I. Hayakawa, *Language in Thought and Action,* 4th ed. (New York: Harcourt Brace Jovanovich, 1978), p. 9.

John McPhee, "Oranges," in William L. Howarth, ed., *The John McPhee Reader* (New York: Vintage, 1978), pp. 75–76.

A. S. Neill, *Summerhill: A Radical Approach to Child Rearing* (New York: Hart, 1960). Quotation from J. M. Wasson, *Subject and Structure,* 6th Ed. (Boston: Little, Brown, 1978), p. 71.

Mark Twain, "Uncle John's Farm." Quotation from J. M. Wasson, *Subject and Structure,* 6th Ed. (Boston: Little, Brown, 1978), p. 71.

James Thurber, from *My Life and Hard Times* (New York: Harper, 1933). Quotation from J. M. Wasson, *Subject and Structure,* 6th Ed. (Boston: Little, Brown, 1978), p. 25.

CHAPTER 11
Percy Bysshe Shelley, *Ode to the West Wind.*

CHAPTER 13

John F. Cragan and Ronald E. Shields, "Communications in American Politics: Symbols Without Substance." Reprinted from *USA Today,* May 1980, p. 62.

CHAPTER 14

John F. Kennedy, "Inaugural Address," *Public Papers of the Presidents of the United States, 1961* (Washington, D.C.: U.S. Government Printing Office, 1962), pp. 1–3.

Abraham Lincoln, "Address at the Dedication of the Gettysburg National Monument."

CHAPTER 15

Gerald Leinwald, *The Traffic Jam* (New York: Washington Square Press, 1969), pp. 24–25.

William McCluskey, "Hard Times Hit the Bay," *National Wildlife,* April–May, 1984, p. 8.

Benjamin Franklin, *The Autobiography of Benjamin Franklin,* as cited in J. M. Wasson, *Subject and Structure,* 8th ed. (Boston: Little, Brown, 1984), p. 367.

Fred R. Oberg, "Safety," *Heavy Timber Construction* (Chicago: American Technical Society, 1963), p. 20.

Victor Cline, *Where Do You Draw the Line: An Exploration of Media Violence, Pornography and Censorship* (Provo, Utah: Brigham Young University Press, 1974), p. ix.

Herbert S. Zim and Robert H. Baker, *Stars: A Guide to the Constellations, Sun, Moon, Planets, and Other Features of the Heavens* (New York: Golden Press, 1956), pp. 20–21.

Narcissa Chamberlain, *The Omelette Book* (New York: Alfred A. Knopf, 1955), pp. 13–14.

Mike Scherer, "Choosing Your Down Sleeping Bag," *Sierra,* March–April, 1984, p. 49.

Peter Farb, *Humankind* (Boston: Houghton Mifflin, 1978), p. 4.

Harold J. Grossman, *Grossman's Guide to Wines, Spirits, and Beers,* 4th ed. (New York: Scribner's, 1964), p. 18.

Helen Curtis, *Biology,* 2nd ed. (New York: Worth Publishers, 1976), p. 565.

Stendhal, *Love* (New York: Penguin, 1982), pp. 73–74.

Bruno Bettelheim, *The Uses of Enchantment: The Meaning and Importance of Fairy Tales* (New York: Alfred A. Knopf, 1976), p. 238.

CHAPTER 16

Carin Rubenstein, "The Future of the Income Hang-Up," *Psychology Today*, November 1982, p. 40.

"Flipping the 50 Billionth Burger," *Time*, Oct. 8, 1984, p. 60.

Claire Safran, "Corporate Women: Just How Far Have We Come?" *Working Woman*, March 1984, p. 99.

Index

261